Cheris

Dream Tomorrow, Live Today

A
AB
ABR
ABRA
ABRAC
ABRACA
ABRACAD
ABRACADA
ABRACADAB
ABRACADABR
ABRACADABRA

ABRACADABRA

Based on the true story
of how one family found the magic in their lives.

by Penny Juros

IN COLLABORATION WITH PAM LAZOS

ISBN: 1-4392-1966-4
ISBN-13: 9781439219669

Visit www.booksurge.com to order additional copies.

Andrea,
Thanks for sharing
the magic.
Penny
2/09

ABRACADABRA

Cherish Yesterday,
Dream Tomorrow, Live Today

DEDICATION

This book is dedicated to the memory of my husband Don.

Don's dying wish was for me to publish our family's story in the hopes that it might support another family as it tackles adversity and challenges. He also hoped that by sharing with others we would continue to "spread the magic".

Don came into my life in 1974, at the age of 15, and departed in 2000, at the age of 41.

He forever will remain my inspiration, guiding light, guardian angel and creator of the magic in my life

With each moment he continues to add the abracadabra to my world.

ACKNOWLEDGMENTS

This book would not have been possible without the love, support and guidance of my parents, Roberta and Jerry Goldberg., my biggest cheerleaders in life.

My unending gratitude also goes to my special friend and confidant, Barbara Wolnerman for always lending her wisdom, ear and heart;

To my friends and family, new and old, who lent me their patience, love and support that helped guide me through my many storms;

To Michael, the new, and hopefully last, love of my life;

To Pam Lazos, for having the talent and creativity to take my pain, tears, loss and writings and transform them into sentences that flow on the paper like magic.

A special acknowledgment goes to Faith, my hero–my normal, practical, stable, rational, beautiful daughter.

And, to Chad: the living manifestation of the word "magic," who taught me that I could get through anything if I would just Say The Magic Word……

Chapter 1

The Luckiest Woman in the World

When anyone would ask me to name the happiest day of my life I would always say May 25, 1988, the day Chad was born. That was the day I felt complete at last. I had all I'd ever wanted since the age of sixteen. I'd married Don, my high school sweetheart, and now we had two children, Faith, just over age two, and Chad. Although I was never very religious at night I'd pray to God and promise that if he'd make my children healthy, we'd make them happy.

Don and I were one of those gaggy couples, inseparable since the age of fifteen. We dated for eight years and married in 1981. It rained; no actually there were torrential downpours, on our wedding day, a beneficent sign, surely good luck everyone said. But they were wrong.

Faith was born in 1986 when Don was in his fourth year of dental school. We were dirt poor in those days, but blissed out on our present lives and our promising, magical future. Chad was born two years later the same weekend Don bought his dental practice. A solo practice was something we'd dreamed of since high school and it was a find. I think we'd looked at every dental practice up and down the East Coast, only to come up empty. It was Don's Dad who found this fully staffed and thriving practice.

We moved to Egg Harbor Township, New Jersey, so Don could be near his new practice and I felt like the luckiest woman in the world, deliriously happy, married to my best friend, my lover, my high school sweetheart. Our life was graced with a simple magic. It seemed that everything we touched turned to gold. We spent the next few years raising our incredibly healthy happy children; all my prayers had been answered. Don was just as involved with raising both Faith and Chad as I was. He would rush home from his office at night wanting to hang with his three favorite pals. Chad and Don were truly best of buds, always hanging together.

Three years later, both our happiness and our luck ran out.

Chapter 2

Me? Smother-Mother?

Labor Day weekend, 1991. Something wasn't right. We just weren't sure what. We were getting away for a much needed four-day excursion. With the new practice and a three and five-year old at home, it was tough and way too expensive to do much more than mini-vacations. One of Don's patients had given him admission tickets to an amusement park and the kids were beside themselves with excitement.

Chad had been sick a lot for the six weeks before and we'd been shuttling him back and forth to the hospital for blood work. Over and over, the results were the same: slightly anemic. Even though it was only a two and a half hour trip from our house to the park, Chad whined the whole way, something unusual for him. Thankfully, his lethargy dissolved and the moment we walked through those gates the flush returned to his cheeks. Still I couldn't lose the feeling that something was out of sorts and said so to Don several times over the course of the day.

We did every inch of that park: rides, water slides, thrill shows, even a petting zoo and collapsed in our hotel room after dinner, sore and exhausted. Don slept in one bed, Faith slept on a cot, and I slept with Chad in another bed. I woke up in the middle of the night thinking how wonderful the heating pad felt on my sore muscles. But then it hit me, I wasn't at home and there wasn't a heating pad, it was Chad, and he was burning up. Don rushed out to an all-night pharmacy to buy medicine and a thermometer. One hundred and three degrees later, I was shaking and very scared.

Chad woke up a new kid the next morning, spunky, energetic and fever free. I was nervous, but decided to play it cool as we spent another fun-filled extravaganza of a day at the park. Sometime in the afternoon, Chad began complaining of leg pain. Since he didn't have a fever, we figured he sprained a muscle from all of the activity. By that time, we were so beat we decided to pack it in for the day and have an early night. The next morning Chad felt punky so instead of another park day we headed for home. At home, Don and the kids played tennis, but when Chad quit after a few minutes due to being so tired, I couldn't take it anymore and called the pediatrician.

Over the next few days, Dr. Gold began a series of even more blood tests and Chad saw an orthopedist for his muscle and hip complaints. The orthopedist said Chad had transient synovitis, commonly known as inflammation of the hip, or growing pains, and that it was common in boys of Chad's age. We had a short-lived period of relief.

Two nights later, Chad woke up drenched in so much sweat it soaked through to his mattress. In the middle of the night, I was washing sheets and changing linens, scared out of my mind. The pediatrician ordered more tests and Chad saw more specialists. One had a preliminary diagnosis of juvenile arthritis, another said polio. More intrusive tests were ordered. Weeks of fevers, needle pricks and negative results followed; the days were getting shorter and colder, and Chad was missing tons of pre-school. I was nuts with worry, but had convinced myself that a cold had settled in Chad's hip and wouldn't let go.

"Pen," Don said. "Let's make a deal. I'll be the designated worrier. You can have five minutes a day and I'll worry the rest of the time. Except for those five minutes and unless I tell you to start, you're off the hook."

Begrudgingly, and to the extent I could, I acquiesced.

Chapter 3

While Visions of Epidurals Danced in Their Heads

As if it was that easy. It was the night before my 34th birthday. I'd gone to bed excited – we had a fun day planned – and woke up screaming, moaning, yelling in my sleep. Don shook me awake.

"Pen, wake up! What's wrong?"

"Oh my God, they were giving Chad an epidural to numb his back. Why are they numbing Chad's back?" I cried to Don, shaking all over. I don't remember sleeping anymore that night.

The dream haunted me all the next morning even while we were getting ready to go to my friend, Laura's, to help her pack to move to her new home.

"C'mon guys, hurry up," I called. "Laura needs more boxes."

"I don't want to go," Chad said. "My leg hurts."

"I know, baby. How about we bring a movie and you can lay and watch it while Faith and I help pack?"

Driving over to Laura's, the vividness of that dream returned again, knocking first on the car window and then later in my mind's eye while at Laura's, knee-deep in boxes. Dr. Gold's return call brought me back to reality.

"Penny, it appears Chad has what they call acute lymphoblastic leukemia, or ALL. I'm having Dr. Robert Wasserman call you. Are you home?"

Leukemia? I collapsed on Laura's bed: "Leukemia? Is that bad?"

Dr. Gold told me to go home and wait for Dr. Wasserman's call which should be soon.

I hung up, shaking, and called Don's office. The receptionist answered.

"Let me talk to Don fast."

"Penny, is that you? You sound funny."

"Let me talk to Don!" I screamed. "Please."

Don came on the line a moment later. "Helloooo. What's up, Pen?"

"Don, my God, Don. Dr. Gold says Chad may have leukemia. Is that a bad thing?"

I heard my husband draw a long deep breath before answering.

"Pen, remember when I told you I'll let you know when it's important enough to worry?"

"Yes." I heard a voice respond, but I couldn't identify it as my own: small, scared, barely a whisper.

"Penny, start worrying."

I started pounding the bed, screaming, heaving, and asking him and God if Chad was going to die. Don's voice came from light years away.

"Listen, babe. I just started a crown preparation. I've already numbed the patient. I've got to finish. I'll be quick. Go home and wait for the doctor to call. Let Faith stay and play. I'll pick her up on my way home"

I left Faith with Laura, grabbed Chad and jumped in my car. They say you go in the zone when you're behind the wheel, that your instincts take over, and that many accidents are avoided because people are in this state of mind. Lucky for Chad and me because I have no recollection of the drive home that day.

I wanted to call my parents, my brother, my sister, Don's parents, anyone who'd tell me that the diagnosis was ludicrous, that it was all a bad dream, that I'd wake up and laugh hysterically with relief. But that was 1991. We didn't even have call waiting yet, let alone a cell phone, and so I sat and waited, and paced and waited, and called Dr. Gold and screamed that no one had called me yet and waited.

Dr. Gold told me I'd get a call as soon as Dr. Wasserman finished his rounds so I called my brother, Mark.

My parents were in Connecticut interviewing for jobs at the casinos, a little something to help them financially in retirement. I knew they were staying at an Inn, but I didn't know if it was a Comfort Inn, Holiday Inn, Hampton Inn, Fairfield Inn or what. Mark found a directory assistance operator who stayed on the line with him, calling every hotel in the area. Hours later, my parents called. My mother was devastated. Forget that they'd both been hired by the casinos for jobs they'd never start. They drove home in record time. My life and the lives of those closest to me were suddenly about to change forever.

Chapter 4

Why I Hate My Birthday

Meanwhile, birthday plans had come to a screeching halt. October 21, 1991 was my 34th birthday and the day our world collapsed. Life for the Juros family would never be the same again.

Chad had always been a healthy kid and didn't get sick often, yet here he was, not with a cold, not an ear infection, but leukemia, oh my God! How could my funny little guy with the adorable smile and the wonderful temperament be diagnosed with such a horrible disease?

By six o'clock I'd already burned the chicken and overcooked the pasta. And the phone was ringing.

"Hello, Mrs. Juros. How are you?" asked Dr. Robert Wasserman, attending oncologist of Children's Hospital of Philadelphia.

"I could be better. You tell me."

"And you'll be better again, I promise. It may not be for a few years, but you will be better," Dr. Wasserman said. "You're lucky to have Children's Hospital of Philadelphia (CHOP) so close. We see about twenty cases a year."

"Twenty? That's it? Are you kidding me? I want to hear hundreds of cases a year. So much information and research that this is no biggee." My stomach was churning, but I kept my voice steady. "Am I close?"

Dr. Wasserman hesitated. "No, I'm sorry. You're not. This is still a rarity and no one knows the whys or hows. What I am offering you is hope."

I was stunned into silence.

"How's Chad now? Any fever?" he asked.

"I don't think so."

"Then stay home tonight. Sleep in your own beds. Meet me at CHOP tomorrow at 8 a.m. and be prepared to stay for three days. We'll want to do a spinal tap, bone marrow aspiration and start Chad on medication. We may even need to do a blood transfusion if necessary."

That was the first of many telephone conversations with Dr. Wasserman's, Chad's primary oncologist. To my amazement, he was right. We were, eventually, better. Before he hung up he gave me his home phone number and told us to call him anytime with questions. He'd meant it, and we did, although I always felt bad for bothering him. And each time, not only did he give us his full attention; he also gave us the ultimate gift: he never lied to us.

I hung up the phone. The room was spinning. I felt like I was going to throw up and grabbed the kitchen counter for support. Faith and Chad were chattering away, their voices a subtle backdrop to the words "spinal tap" that reverberated in my brain, over and over, like the distant beat of war drums. There's the epidural I dreamt about the night before. Talking about living a dream. Only it wasn't a dream, it was more like a nightmare.

Don and I barely slept. We clung to each other all night, crying, analyzing, and dissecting our lives, looking for the source of this trouble. Were we being punished? We were such a tight, loving family, so why us? When Chad was conceived, we lived in Brick, New Jersey. Brick, along with Toms River, has informally become known as "the cancer cluster" due to the alarmingly high rate of children with cancers coming out of this area. When Chad was born we were living in a condominium complex that bordered a stream into which toxins were/had been dumped. The condo unit treated our grass with pesticides frequently; while I was pregnant they painted our unit. All these factors pointed to the creation of a potentially weakened immune system in utero which resulted in

Chad's diagnosis later. But there was no way to know for sure.

We spent hours covering the same ground, pointing fingers, exhausting ourselves in the search for clues. What did we finally conclude? Self-analysis is good to a point; self-effacing and self-deprecation during times of crisis is a serious waste of time. But we were Jewish, and like every believer in a guilt-based religion, we first needed to spend the hours thrashing ourselves to bits with the weight of it all before we could refocus on what positive things we could do. It was what it was and now we needed to figure out what to do with it. Easier said than done.

My parents came at 6:30 the next morning. My dad drove us to CHOP and my mom stayed home to put Faith on the school bus. The whole ride up Don and my dad sat in the front seat making small talk. I sat in the back with Chad on my lap and tears streaming down my face, scared witless.

At the hospital we walked around in a daze. It's when we got off at the fourth floor that the horror started. This was the oncology unit and everywhere you looked there were little bald-headed kids, some with feeding tubes up their noses, others attached to poles with wires and tubes. One look and I started gagging. Then I grabbed Don's hand and started begging.

"Please. Let's get out of here. Chad doesn't belong here. This is a mistake. Take us home."

I collapsed to the floor and buried my face in my knees. If I could have hidden away from the nightmare around me I would have. But when I opened my eyes, the images were still there, surrounding me in all their brilliant Technicolor.

A lifetime later, they called our name. I cried through the entire exchange of information, names, dates, diseases, insurance carriers, all necessary yet ridiculous in comparison to the very visceral information swirling around in my head and solar plexus. Something terrible was about to happen to my baby and I was powerless to stop it.

The kind receptionist patted my hand and said, "I wish you strength."

It's funny, in life's most erratic and stressed times, the moments you remember.

Chapter 5

Let Me Count to Three

They brought us to triage, took Chad's height and weight and had him sit on my lap for the fun part: the first of quite possibly a bazillion needles he's been stuck with so far this lifetime.

"Let me count to three. When I say three, you jab me," he said to the triage nurse. My baby. What a trooper.

After the procedure I stood up and said, "We're done, right? He's better? We can go home. Whatever you just did fixed him, right? So we're out of here?"

The phlebotomist took my hand and said, "You poor thing."

Five minutes later, Dr. Wasserman entered the waiting room and introduced himself. I was shocked. I couldn't believe this was the same guy I talked to on the phone the night before.

"No offense," I said, "but you're too young. I want an old wise doctor with tons of experience with this diagnosis. You aren't experienced enough for us."

Dr. Wasserman explained that he was an attending physician and his expertise was in leukemia and that Chad was in the best possible care at CHOP. I was skeptical, I was adamant, and I was totally against it, but there was something in his manner, so I relented. It was probably one of the best decisions I've ever made.

Dr. Wasserman explained that in order to confirm Chad's diagnosis they needed to do a bone marrow aspiration. Basically, they stick a long needle into Chad's hip bone and withdraw fluid or marrow. Just the thought caused my stomach to lurch.

"Does it hurt?" I asked.

"Yes," Dr. Wasserman said. "It's actually very painful, but we put a numbing medicine on the site first to alleviate some of the pain."

Chad started crying. "I don't want anymore needles today. No more. We'll come back. Please, Mommy."

Dr. Wasserman told us to take a moment to collect our thoughts and he'd meet us in the procedure room. The minute he left, I fell into Don's arms.

"Let's just go, Don. Chad's right. We'll come back. Look how much better he looks already. Maybe it went away. Maybe they had a mix-up in the lab and tested the wrong blood. Maybe we can wait. Please don't let them hurt our baby."

One look at Don's face told me he was barely holding it together himself. He looked haggard, distraught and thoroughly beaten. The only reason he was still standing was because of me and Chad.

So I got a grip. I realized then that it doesn't help to cry and beg and plead and make deals with God or whoever – although I can't say I gave up that behavior completely over the years – but it does help to use humor.

So we did. Don and I started joking with Chad, trying to bring him around, make light of the situation.

When they laid him on the gurney Chad said, "Just show me everything and tell me everything you're going to do, okay? Explain it to me. No surprises."

I laughed out loud. This from a three-year old. He sounded like his father, taking control where he could.

The needle was about as big as he was.

While they were prepping him for the aspiration, Don, *The Great Donaldo* as he was also known, focused Chad's attention by doing magic tricks. Chad was transfixed as magic was one of Chad's favorite hobbies he enjoyed performing with his dad. Don was always spending time with Chad teaching him magic tricks. Even Dr. Wasserman and the nurses watched the floor show while I sat in the corner with a stupid nervous smile plastered on my face, thinking, Shouldn't we be freaking out here? Am I the only sane one or the nut?"

A few minutes later, Dr. Belinda Long, world-renowned, number one, best-in-the-business, walked into the procedure room. She introduced herself and asked if we had any questions.

"Only about nine million," I said, "first and foremost being, will Chad live?"

"We've made amazing strides in the world of leukemia research," she said. "Children are living today much more so than ever."

"Yeah, but what about Chad?"

"Chad has a seventy percent chance of survival."

Seventy percent!" My heart seized up. Seventy percent was too low.

Chapter 6

Where I Repeat Myself

Seventy percent? Oh my God, seventy percent. I'm crying, begging, only seventy percent? There's got to be a mistake. Seventy percent?

Thankfully, Dr. Long resisted whatever urge she may have had to slap me across the face *a la* Cher and Nicholas Cage in *Moonstruck.* Instead she replied:

"Mrs. Juros, today seventy percent is incredible odds. We'll do everything in our power to have Chad be one of the survivors."

My peripheral vision registered my husband across the room still performing magic for Chad while various hospital personnel looked on, but paroxysms of fear had wrapped themselves around my leg muscles and despite my commands, they did little more than shake. Minutes later our new normal, the world of needles poked into hips and spines and arms, the world of finger pricks and x-rays, the world of pure horror and worry had begun.

When the terrifying procedure was over I excused myself to go to the ladies room for the umpteenth time to fix my face and pull myself together. Streaks of tears had left tracks of dissolved make-up on my cheeks. One look in the mirror and I was shocked at the image staring back: a haggard, pale and hopeless wreck. A woman in the bathroom noticed my demeanor and took pity on me.

"It's not so bad, really it isn't. You learn to live with it and it becomes second nature." She touched my shoulder. "Your son will be fine. One of the lucky ones. He has a lot of love and support."

After she left, I cried. How could she say that? How was it possible that anything this horrible could become second nature?

When Dr. Wasserman came back from checking on the blood test results he confirmed that Chad had acute lymphoblastic leukemia, ALL.

"Tomorrow we'll hold a family meeting. We'll explain the course of treatment for the next three years," Dr. Wasserman said. "Now we need to admit Chad as an in-patient, order him a blood transfusion, and start him on some medicine."

Blood transfusion. He said it as calmly as if he were calling out for Chinese food.

"Is it our fault because we took him to an amusement park and put him in a crowd of people when he didn't have much of an immune system?" a ridiculous question, I knew, but no more ridiculous than the set of facts with which Dr. Wasserman had just presented me.

"No, Penny," he replied. "It's no one's fault. You did nothing wrong. Focus on what you can and have done right."

Minutes later, a wheelchair arrived and a nurse who introduced herself as Debbie said to Chad, "You're chariot awaits."

"Cool," he said, and jumped on.

Chad was happy, but my record started skipping again. "Debbie, they say my son has leukemia. Is it a mistake? Could it be a mistake? Is it my fault because we took him to an amusement park?" On and on I rambled, repeating the same phrases over and over, looking for the magic bullet that would kill the monster, rid Chad of the disease and let us go home. My search yielded nothing but sympathetic smiles and uncomfortable silences.

We took the elevator, following Chad's wheelchair like pups after their mother.

"This is Seven East," Debbie says. "The oncology ward. We treat all types of cancers here at CHOP."

"But Chad has leukemia," I said. "They told you the wrong floor, Debbie. You made a mistake. My son doesn't have cancer."

Debbie took my hand. "Mrs. Juros, fasten your seatbelt. You're in for the ride of your life."

The spigot opened up again. There was nothing I could say. I pounced on the only one I could, my husband.

My words poured out in hysteria and fury. "Don, they made a mistake. They said Chad has cancer. No one said leukemia was cancer. How can it be cancer? How can our baby have cancer? He's only three. Such a good boy, cheerful, happy. He can't have cancer. Cancer is for people who'll die. Chad can't die. He didn't do anything wrong, Don. Tell them. Go tell them they made a mistake."

I was screaming, crying, squeezing him so hard, trying to keep myself from spinning off into an alternate universe, but Don's face told me I was wrong and that they weren't all nuts at this crazy hospital. He wouldn't meet my gaze, just held me in his arms and cried along with me. After what seemed like days, but was probably minutes, we pulled ourselves together.

They put us in a hospital room with a boy Chad's age; only the poor child was bald, very pale and swollen. His face looked blown up and his little arms and chest had pumps and wires stuck everywhere. There was even a tube inserted in his nose.

Now I'm not a bad person. But when I'm scared, the bitch in me comes out. Like any mother protecting her young, I'd claw your eyes out before I'd let you hurt my baby. And in my brain's altered stage, I perceived the child in that bed with his swollen body and bowling ball head to be a threat to my family's continued health and happiness – and a possible mirror to our future.

I walked by like I'm the coolest thing in the world. *Ha. I have no idea what your son's diagnosis is, but my son has leukemia and he doesn't look like a monster so I guess I'm better than you are so there,* I said to myself.

The mom and dad were laughing, watching cartoons with the little boy. I walked to my side of the room and pulled the curtain across.

"Are these people crazy?" I whispered to Don. "They're laughing and acting normal. Have we entered the twilight zone?"

I crossed the room to use the bathroom. The woman smiled at me, but I looked the other way. If I'm not looking it won't happen. *I don't want your mirror, baby.* On my way back she's standing at the door. She introduced herself and told me her son had leukemia. I wanted to die. Before my eyes, the mirror was splintering into a million tiny fragments all with the face of my own bald-headed baby.

Inside my head I'm screaming: *No way, please God, no way. Don't tell me Chad is going to look like that one day.* Outside I'm cool and confident and almost snobby.

"Well, he might have leukemia, but my son has ALL. He's got a seventy percent cure rate." *Ha. Take that.* I thought so smugly.

Wouldn't you know it. That oh-so-kind woman replies, "So does mine."

Aaggggghhhhhhh. I drew a tortured breath and then another. It couldn't have been harder to breathe if someone had sprayed caulk in my lungs. Chad and his roommate, Chuck, were chatting. Sure enough, they were the same age with the same birthday. Was this some kind of bad practical joke? The parallels were killing me; I wanted to throw up.

The parents of this monster child were lovely and educated and kind. I wanted them to be degenerates, pedophiles, drug addicts, anything to separate them from us, to prove their child *deserved* it. Wrong again.

A parade of doctors, nurses and specialists had all begun to arrive, asking the same questions, repeating the same procedures, looking at Chad's chart, checking his vital signs. I told each of them how lousy a birthday it was, how horrible a present this was. I tried to extract promises for a good outcome, more years for my son, pleading on Chad's behalf. If they thought I was crazy, they didn't let on, but kept telling me we were one of the lucky ones and how good Chad's chances of survival were.

I thought that if this was good luck I better never see bad. But this wasn't lucky. Lucky were the kids playing outside in the park, swinging on the swings and playing in the sandbox, the kids who were going to sleep at home in their own beds tonight. Lucky were not the kids getting spinal taps and bone marrow aspirations. That's not lucky, that's hell.

I started another round of *why us?* It would by no means be my last.

Why us, we were so much in love, high school sweethearts, the envy of all our friends. What happened to the deal, "you make them healthy, we'll make them happy"? Why was God so angry with us?

I collapsed in my chair which I'd later find opened to a bed. Little did I know how many nights I'd spend sleeping on it. Welcome to Penny's pity party.

Chapter 7

Don't Let Those Doors Close

The one good thing that's come out of all this – if good is a term that can even be used to classify such life-altering experiences – is that I've learned to throw off anxiety the way you throw off the bed sheets in the morning: up and at 'em and on with the business of life. It used to take me much longer, huddling in the proverbial corner for hours or days whining, *why us*, and wondering how we'd ever pull through. But when you've watched loved ones suffer as much as I have, when you've lost so much of all you've held dear, you come to the realization that there is no time for cowering or huddling, only for living. And although its cliché, I've come to know on a visceral level the meaning of the words *all we have is the present.*

Still, those were the fledgling days and I hadn't yet perfected my techniques. It was the first day and there was much to learn about the enemy we were fighting, but it was late and we hadn't eaten all day.

Chad was practically doing back flips because there was a McDonald's in the lobby. Not only could he have a happy meal every day, but he could watch his own TV with his own VCR and not have to share with his sister.

"Faith is going to be so jealous," he said. "This is the coolest place in the world, huh Mom?"

If they cured him I promised myself I wouldn't disagree.

"Why don't you get going, Babe?" I said to Don. "Faith's going to be missing everyone and you guys both need to get ready for school and work tomorrow." The thought of attending to such mundane tasks as school and work when our whole world had shifted a dozen degrees to chaos seemed almost ludicrous, but as anyone who's suffered through a trauma of such magnitude knows, it's the routine that keeps your head from flying off.

Don kissed Chad and hugged him like he had never before, as if he would never again. He was crying and taking deep breaths and my heart was expanding with all the love and compassion I had for my two men although at the time it was hard to tell the difference between love and cardiac arrest. Maybe another person would have asked for a drink, a sedative, something to numb the pain, but I needed to be clear-headed for Chad and thought that by staying with my own pain, I could process some of Chad's for him. To my mind, hope and pain had become interchangeable.

I walked Don to the elevator and the cloak of anxiety that I'd managed to shove in the corner of our hospital room caught up with me in the hall, and wrapped me in a stranglehold, its eager grip around my chest and neck, throttling the hell out of me.

I started crying, talking nonsensical stuff while anxiety tried suffocating me, looking for the takedown. "Maybe we should just let him die, save him any pain. Why make him suffer if he might die anyway? Tell them to let him die so he doesn't have to get anymore needles. Please, Don."

Don gripped my arms and looked me in the eye. "Penny, get a hold of yourself. We have a lot of hope. No one's dying. We'll do everything the doctors tell us. Chad will be a survivor, okay? Have I ever lied to you before?"

I shook my head.

"I promise you, Pen, Chad will be okay."

The elevator doors opened. Don kissed me and walked inside.

I started screaming. "Don, take us with you. Don't you dare leave us here. We've never been apart.

Please. We need to come home with you now, Don. Please don't let those doors close."

The doors closed in my face.

I pounded on them, begging the cold, smooth steel surface to open up, let us in.

"Please open the doors. Don't leave us, Donny-babe. Don't leave us. Take us home."

The doors were unmoved by my pleas. I collapsed to the lobby floor exhausted.

Anxiety had won this round. I immediately thought of my Faith, my daughter, my normal. Life would never be normal again for her or any of us.

Chapter 8

Only Thirty-One Pills a Day

I brushed myself off and sauntered back to our prison cell as if screaming at elevator doors was an everyday occurrence for me. Thank God it was late, around 10 PM, and there were very few people around to witness my complete emotional breakdown.

My mood shifted when I saw Chad. He was truly enjoying this experience. It ended abruptly when the nurse tried to get him to take some pills – thirty-one, to be exact – and Chad refused. They switched to a liquid chemo which he still wouldn't take. It took several of us holding him down while I squeezed the medicine into the sides of his mouth, hoping he wouldn't spit it out. *How the heck was I going to do this by myself when we got home?* Our first five days of treatment had begun. Within two hours, Chad was vomiting so the nurses decided to put an IV in his arm to administer the chemo.

He finally fell asleep. Not me, though. I kept running the tape, rewinding, replaying: *Why me? Why us? What did I do wrong? How can I fix it?* I curled up in a ball and held myself and made a million dumb deals with God. *I promise I won't drive fast. I promise I'll go to synagogue every week, do more charity work, and never take the kids to a crowded amusement park, whatever you want, just ask.* If God wanted in on the bargain he wasn't saying.

Sleep proved elusive so I paced the halls. The rooms were dark and eerily quiet. Where were all the parents of these kids and how could they sleep? I stopped every nurse unfortunate enough to be on duty that night, firing my unanswerable questions at them. "Will my son live? Will he be okay? Is leukemia bad?"

I was still looking for the one person who'd give me the sword with which to slay the beast, or barring that, to shake me, wake me, tell me it's all a joke, a bad dream, go home and live your life.

I checked on Chad a million times during that sleepless night, pacing until about 4 AM.

Then I started calling friends, relatives, links to the other world – the one without needles and bald freak children and dark hospital corridors – searching for hope, anecdotes, a piece of string to grasp onto as I jumped into the void. It was my third night without sleep; there was a dark, blurry smudge where reality used to be.

Chapter 9

And Spinal Taps on Wednesday

Acute lymphoblastic leukemia, or ALL, is a cancer which affects the body's white blood cells, the ones that fight infections. This fast-growing cancer strips the body of its lymphocytes which are the body's inherent defenses, the sentinels that guard the gates, protecting the body from disease. The result is a defenseless and a weakened immune system susceptible to infections that happen across its path. The common cold may result in pneumonia; chicken pox in death. Similar to HIV or other auto-immune diseases that attack the body's immune system, if left untreated ALL will kill you, but it is also a possibility that one of the myriad infections that the body is no longer able to fight will get you first.

About 30 cases per million are diagnosed every year primarily in patients two to twelve years of age. And while environmental factors have been investigated, the actual cause of the disease is still unknown which makes treatment fundamentally a guessing game.

This was the breadth and scope of the monster we were fighting.

Don came back early the next morning with fresh clothes, some games and toys for Chad and a few magic tricks. Both our parents arrived soon after. Don's father held his son's arm and wailed; my mother-in-law cried quietly. The nurse came to take Chad for x-rays and the six of us attended a family meeting with Dr. Wasserman to find out what our future held.

More hell, apparently. For the next three years Chad would be on a protocol of chemotherapy both orally and through the blood stream. He'd get spinal taps on Wednesdays so they could inject chemotherapy right into his spine and every so many weeks he would have to have a bone marrow aspiration to check if he were still in remission. And there were the blood transfusions, outpatient visits, and for now, no school because he didn't have an immune system to speak of. Lucky I was sitting down because my knees had suddenly become like jelly, rendering them a useless body part.

Dr. Wasserman continued that one of the parents would have to be the primary care giver and the other the bread winner. He told us they had new medicines, new treatments, and about how Chad's risk was so much lower than so many others. Instead of being buoyed by these statistics, I was more disheartened than ever.

For five days we were confined to Seven East. I couldn't wait until Friday. The chemo would be over and we'd be sprung, out of there, home to New Jersey, home to my Faith. I knew in my heart that I'd take such good care of Chad that he'd never be an inpatient again. He'd be the miracle. How naive I was.

Each night Chad would sleep and I would lay awake exhausted, mentally and physically drained, praying and making deals with God. Each day I would eagerly wait to hear Faith's voice chattering about school and what she would be wearing tomorrow. I made her lunch – by phone, picked out her clothes – by phone. Faith's needs were being met by either my parents or the phone wires.

On day five we were eagerly awaiting Don's arrival, like the knight in shining armor, he would come to deliver us from our worries and pains and lousy views of the parking lot. He was going to get us out of here.

Don was due at 11 AM. At 10:45 AM, the nurse came in to check Chad's vitals and give us discharge instructions, prescriptions, information on follow up visits. I signed my name on the line. We were free.

Of course you can guess what happened next.

Bam. Out of nowhere, Chad registers a fever of 102.4.

"Sorry, Mrs. Juros. You may as well unpack. You can't go anywhere with a fever like that."

I felt like someone had punched me in the belly. *We couldn't go home.* Nor did we go the next day, or the day after that. It took Chad so long to adjust to the meds that we didn't go home for an entire month.

I became a Stepford mom. I ate what they told me, when they told me, and slept when they told me, that is, when I felt safe enough to close my eyes for ten minutes. I was a living robot.

Over breakfast one morning as Chad took a bite of his cereal a giant clump of hair plopped into the bowl. My baby's hair was falling out in big patches and he looked like and old man.

No, he looked worse, he looked like all those little bald kids we saw on the first day, swollen-faced and pale, kids with cancer.

Chapter 10

Social Butterfly

I couldn't be a Stepford mom forever. I was still a bit shell-shocked, but the sting of the diagnosis was leaving me. We soldiered on and I took control in little ways, looking after Chad like a mother hen, monitoring what the nurses and docs were doing, assuring he was fed and cared for, asking relevant questions, and doing for Faith and Don what I could from the hospital.

As a result, pretty soon I'd adjusted to in-patient life. My lost personality resurfaced and I became a social butterfly. I made friends with all the other parents, both moms and dads and even grandparents. I befriended the orderlies, the nurses, the food-servers and docs. I had Chad's schedule down pat, knew when we went to the playroom, when we needed to be back for chemo, when Chad needed his vitals checked. I became a sponge, learning so much about leukemia and the other cancers, and I realized the docs were right. Where so many kids came in and never left, we had a lot of hope.

I learned the meaning of the terms, I learned what the drugs did, and I even learned how to properly spell the achingly long diagnosis. After our kids went to bed at night, a bunch of us distraught, sleep-deprived parents would congregate in the halls and do whatever we could to release some of our stress. We laughed, shared our painful stories, and pretended we were on tropical islands and this was a vacation. Who wanted to cook and clean at home anyway when this was so much more relaxing?

Everyday, UPS delivered more toys and gifts for Chad. They didn't take the pain away, but they were a necessary distraction. And everyday friends and family would call to let me cry and vent. Don and I only saw each other on Wednesdays and weekends when he'd come to the hospital and sleep in the playroom. It was on these days Don would sit with Chad for hours showing him magic tricks and watching movies with Chad. Chad grew more swollen and pale-faced by the day, still vomiting and completely bald.

We had to force him to eat and when he did he craved weird salty foods like pickles and corned beef. He had tremendous mood swings because of the steroids and either slept too much or not at all. I'd trained myself to survive on four hours sleep a night – and that was a good night. Lying in my hospital chair I'd write to relieve the stress, to keep my dreams alive, if only on paper.

Outside Chad's hospital room window was a helicopter pad with flashing lights. I used to pretend that the light had magical powers and I would pray to the flicker all the time. On one occasion the nurses asked if they could change Chad's room for the evening. I said, "No, I'm sorry. If I don't have that light to pray to then my hope will diminish. As long as I can see the light flickering I know there's hope for Chad." Even as the words came out of my mouth I know they sounded ludicrous. I'd become like a card shark or a horse player with my lucky coins and socks and superstitions – except I was praying to landing pad lights. I'm not ashamed of it. I blame it on anxiety, that Muse of Madness, who caused me to twist my behavior patterns to routinized, yet totally unrecognizable practices. Besides, the nurses were used to it. Every other parent on the floor behaved equally as idiosyncratically.

I wasn't able to see Faith often because she was afraid to come to the hospital, but there was no way I was leaving Chad. He was so vulnerable. Everyday I check and double checked his meds and hovered about the room, keeping all unwanted influences out in the hall. We passed an entire month in this pattern, like two survivors of a shipwreck, until Chad's fever and blood levels were finally stable.

I was petrified, didn't want to leave my safe haven, my new best buddies. No way could I handle this alone at home. What if he spiked a fever? What if he threw up his chemo? What if someone brought a germ into the house? *What if I couldn't do it?*

Little did I know that the biggest obstacle to my success was going to be Chad himself.

Chapter 11

Quit Squirming Or I'll Call The Cops!

"Chad lay still. I can't get this medicine in you if you're going to keep squirming and I can't keep fighting you three times a day over it so either you take it or I'm going to go across the street and get the policeman to come over and make you take it." The Sheriff of Atlantic County did, in fact, live across the street from us and when Chad was little he was petrified of him. Still, it was a feeble threat, I knew, but none of the others had worked yet either. For his part, Chad was unphased. "Don't' you dare spit it out on my couch! Do you think I didn't see you spit it into the napkin? Do you want to get better or what? Would you stop giving me a hard time and cooperate, please?"

And so it went, Chad's regiment of thirty-one pills, three times a day, trips to CHOP three times a week for blood checks, IV and chemotherapy, and of course, the spinal taps once a week. Chad stayed perfectly still while chemo was injected into his back and as the numbing medication took effect Don would work his magic.

Chad had his favorite toys, his favorite nurse, his Dad's magic. All they had to do was talk him through the procedure and count to three and he never complained. He was getting a reputation for being the brave fun guy because there was always a magic trick to be performed in the procedure room. The nurses took to calling him *Magical Chad.*

One day in the playroom they were doing an art project and Chad drew a freehand picture of Mickey Mouse, on steroids, performing magic. The play therapist was so impressed she hung it on her door and because of it, he was asked to participate in the hospital's art show. The kid was only four! He drew a huge lion. Years later, Mickey's was still hanging on the therapist's door and the lion is the first thing you see when you enter the treatment center at CHOP.

Chapter 12

Mommy, Wake Up!

"Mommy, come here. Mommy, wake up. Mommy, please come here," I heard in my dreams. And in my dreams I said to myself, "I hear Chad crying for help. He's in pain and he's crying for me." I snapped up in bed and it hit me – this was real.

I shook Don awake and rushed into Chad's room. He was lying in bed crying and a quick check to his head told me he was burning up with fever. We called the oncologist at CHOP who said to bring him to our local hospital where the docs asked a bunch of questions. The resident seemed baffled by the diagnosis and asked me to spell leukemia. Chad had a fever of 102.7. Confidence in the process was not a phrase I'd use to describe the scenario at that moment.

The resident called the doctors at CHOP who wanted to see Chad immediately, no time to pack even a bag. An hour later we were racing through the halls of the ER ward. Chad's fever had inched up to

103.2 and a new series of tests were run. Don brought us clothes, toys, and of course magic the next morning and a month later we were still inpatients as the antibiotics floating around in Chad's little body did there best to throw off a series of infections and pneumonia.

Poor Faith. I was there to tuck her in and kiss her good night and abracadabra, like magic, I was gone in the morning. In time she became fearful to go to bed at night, fearful I would abandon her. She would ask me over and over "do you promise to be here when I wake up in the morning, Mommy?", or "do you promise to be here when I come home from school today?" She didn't trust me not to disappear and I couldn't promise her I wouldn't.

Chad spent the month in a state of lethargy, Don and I in breathless anxiety. Don resumed his twice weekly visitation, Wednesdays and weekends, and Faith who was still terrified of catching Chad's disease, or worse, something from another child, still refused to come. It was heartbreaking not to see her, but what could I do? Our lives were back to tilt and whirl, the balance severely off.

With spring came chicken pox, but it may as well have been the plague. Chicken pox can be deadly to a person with no immune system and as a first-grader, Faith was exposed often, resulting in Chad's isolation – or rather Faith's. With each exposure we'd have to ship her off to friends or relatives for three weeks at a pop just to keep her apart from her brother.

Which, truth be told, was probably one of the hardest parts of Chad's illness: watching my daughter grow from a distance. I was so overwhelmed with Chad; it left barely an afternoon for Faith. What five-year old shouldn't be allowed to have a friend over for fear of the germs they might be carrying? Or shouldn't be allowed to go to a party because chicken pox was going around? I was always so sad to leave her so I could be with Chad at the hospital. How come for three straight years the Chanukah show and Passover Seder at her school, the Hebrew Academy, were always on the days Chad was scheduled for a spinal? I missed every one of her shows for those three years and my heart fractured a little more every time.

But that's where my parents stepped in. From the minute Chad was diagnosed, they picked up the slack, being there for Faith so Don and I could be there for Chad. They put their lives on hold, suspending their retirement in order to rescue me, and with each new upheaval, they'd disassemble what had become their new life to fit ours in all its varying, shattered degrees.

It had finally gotten so bad that my parents announced they were moving. I couldn't believe they were deserting me at a time like this! Of course they weren't. They ended up moving from their house at the beach – twenty minutes from mine and some prime real estate – to within a mile of us in order to give Faith some normalcy in her life.

"This way she can get on the school bus at our house," my mother said. "Her routine won't be any more upset than it has been and she can still play with the same friends."

I can't tell you how many times that move saved my sanity and our family.

Chapter 13

Okay, I'll Go On One Condition

"Faith, please, I beg you. Come with Daddy to the hospital to visit Mommy and Chad, please. I want so badly to be a family today," Don begged. "Please, Faither
(Don's pet name for her), please."

"No way. Don't make me go. I'll sit in the car in the parking lot and Mommy can come visit me there. Don't you make me go to that place with all those bald kids with those scary tubes. No."

She was adamant, but we found she could be persuaded – for a price.

"How about if I get Mommy and Chad to come downstairs away from that floor? Will you come please?"

"Can we stop off on the way home and get a puppy?"

Don sighed. As if he needed one more thing to take care of.

"If Mommy says we can have a puppy then sure, we'll go pick out a puppy."

So we had lunch together as a family for the first time in eons in the hospital's cafeteria, and on the way home Faith and Don stopped at the Humane Society and got *Muffin*, a miniature poodle and soon the family favorite. Muffin was never as happy as when she was sitting on your lap, being hugged and kissed which was almost always since that's what everyone did with her. She took the edge off our daunting reality and given that dogs are hardwired that way, to love unconditionally, it wasn't even a hard task for her. Finally, someone in our family was having fun and with her, a little light and levity was granted the rest of us.

Chapter 14

Goodbye, I Hope to Never See You Again

Days turned into seasons and one day winter was so entrenched, even Don got to enjoy a snow day. So what did The Great Donaldo do with his newfound time?

"Get dressed kids. We're going sledding."

"Don, Chad's ability to fight infection is zip. He'll get damp, catch a chill, then a cold, and boom; we're in the hospital for three weeks."

"Penny, *you* chill. I'm taking my son sledding. I might never have this opportunity again."

That broke my heart, knowing that Don feared a future without his son. I shut my mouth and opened the door. I looked out the living room window every three and a half seconds for the next two hours, enough to almost give me whiplash while the living room carpet had developed a noticeable groove from my pacing. *We were going to pay for this.* I was getting ready to do a drive-by, to cruise the local sledding hills, looking for familiar hats and gloves, when Don's car pulled in the driveway and the kids came running in with lunch. They couldn't get to me quick enough.

"Mommy, that was the best day ever," Chad said. We made snow angels and went sledding."

"You weren't cold?"

"Babe, you'd have been so proud of me," Don said. "I took my socks off and put them on Chad's hands for extra warmth."

There's a Jewish word for when you get so choked up emotionally about something they can't say a word in response. Talk about *vaklempt*!

Years later, I found out the woman in the bathroom had been right. Cancer had become a way of life for us, not one we were defenseless against, rather one we had learned to cohabitate with, perhaps not always peaceably, but at least not always with guns drawn. Don had changed his entire work schedule so he could be home every evening for dinner with us as well as on weekends. He never worked a minute more than he had to.

"Pen, are the bills being paid?"

"Yes, but it's tight."

"That's not what I asked you. I asked you, as my office manager, if there was enough money to keep a roof over our heads, to put food on our table and gas in our car, to pay for Chad's medicine. I need to spend all but the minimum amount of time necessary to earn a living, with my family."

"I agree, but why are you so pessimistic? Do you question Chad's chances to be a survivor? Don't you feel hope?"

"I don't question it, Pen. But whether it is Chad, Faith, you or even me, who knows what the future holds. I'm just trying to capture as much of the magic as I can while I can."

And he did. Don was the magician at Faith's seventh birthday party. The children were enthralled and Faith was so proud of him. He did so much with his kids, always making time to talk at their school about dentistry or teach them to ride bikes and play tennis. Faith and Don built a dollhouse from scratch; with Chad he built rockets. They watched homemade movies and staged little plays and laughed so hard they probably could have squirt soda out their noses. Don would take Chad golfing and let him drive the cart. They put on magic shows for Chad's friends.

And thank God, because as they were, future was once again, restructuring itself into something unrecognizable, and once again, we never even saw it coming.

Finally, the day arrived. December 1, 1994. After three years of emergency hospital stays, home care, chemotherapy, and spinal taps, Chad was done, finished with his leukemia treatments. He had tolerated the chemo well and his remission seemed assured, another childhood cancer success story. We'd made it, crossed the finish line, and bought our lives back. Dr. Wasserman had promised me life would be good again and he was right. I regained my crowned title of *Luckiest Woman in the World.* The docs gave us our discharge papers with instructions to go live our lives to the fullest.

As we were getting in the elevator we saw one of Chad's original doctors. I hugged her and said, "Goodbye. We hope we never see you again."

So many didn't get to leave that place alive, but here we were, walking, well actually racing out the door. We stopped at the magic store in Philadelphia, and giggled the whole way home to get Faith.

Finally, we were going to have a night out, away from the hospital, together as a family again. So why wasn't Don as excited as I thought he would be?

Chapter 15

Can Anyone Say, Shifting Sand?

It was November 1995, and we'd spent the last year doing exactly as we'd been told, living life to the fullest. We took at least five different vacations – Philadelphia, New York, Colorado, Arizona, Florida – visiting friends and relatives across the country, back to the world of beaches and parades, circuses and crowds, all those activities that required an immune system. Chad had reclaimed his and we weren't beyond flaunting it. Everyone wanted a piece of our miracle; it was only right to share.

Chad was enrolled in first grade, finally healthy enough to attend school. Faith was in third grade. Both joined the baseball teams and went to camp for the entire summer.

Mrs. House, Chad's first grade teacher, and later his homebound teacher, told me Chad was the comedian of the class, always happy, smiling and silly.

Everyday after school when the bus rolled in, Chad would either have his lips pressed against the window or his fingers up his nose or his eyes screwed up, anything to make me laugh. One particular day though this was not so.

Uh oh. Chad is never not happy.

"What happened?" I asked as he came running off the bus. He burst into tears, so hysterical he couldn't catch his breath. "What? What?" I said, hoping my voice belied the panic.

"I got detention."

Mrs. House had flagged him for goofing off, getting out of his seat too much and generally playing the class clown. While the words crawled out of Chad's mouth, all garbled and grim, I resisted the urge to burst out laughing. This was hot news and I couldn't wait to spread it. *Hallelujah.* Truly a Hallmark moment.

I called Don at work (out of Chad's earshot, of course) and we laughed until we cried.

"That's great, Babe," he said. Finally – we've got a normal healthy kid."

More evidence that life had settled into a pleasant buzz of routine.

Except that Don wasn't buzzing. Rather than eagerly traipsing around the countryside with his family, he preferred the quiet and solitude of home. And he didn't know why. We saw a few doctors, trying to make sense of what was happening. The doctors attributed his symptoms to post traumatic stress syndrome.

It didn't make sense to either of us. Yeah, we'd been through it, but it was over now and life was pretty darn good again. Yet here was Don, Dr. Rational, Dr. Practical, Dr. Healthy, falling apart. My rock was crumbling before my eyes. And while I'd witnessed the myriad ways people deal with their stresses while living with a cancer child – fallen marriages, drug and alcohol abuse, sex addictions, all placebos for the pain – I never in a million years expected that kind of aberrant behavior from my husband.

"But why now?" I asked. "What's up with you? What about living life to the fullest? We brought home the miracle, got exactly what we prayed for. So why don't you trust our good?"

And you know what that man said? That strong, handsome, brave, practical, always-in-control man? The man I confided all to, depended completely upon, the man who weighed in on any topic even mildly relevant to our better well being? Do you know what he said?

Nothing. Just stared off into space without a word for me.

Here was my response in descending order: irate; annoyed; concerned. Well, less concerned, more irate and annoyed. So I quipped, because I always quipped when life was about to beat the bloody hell out of me:

"Have your nervous breakdown another time, Don. Now you need to get a grip."

And he did. Just like that. All of a sudden as if I'd flipped a switch. It was maddening in that it happened again and again. So perhaps it wasn't much of a surprise to me later when the sands did their eroding and magical disappearing acts again.

Chapter 16

But In The Meantime...

Thanksgiving had always been my favorite holiday. We'd invite the whole family over, all twenty-one of them, and sit around, sampling ample portions of fall delicacies and wrap it all up with a birthday celebration for Don and his Mom. Thanksgiving 1995 we had more to be thankful for than usual so I'd planned a full out, gloves off, no-holds-barred kind of celebration.

The Monday before turkey day, Chad woke up with a runny nose. I thought nothing of it. In the past when Faith was sick we'd poo-poo it, give her medicine and watch it go away. She was our normal child. Not so with Chad, of course, so I'd find ways to assess his state of health without alarming him: kissing him, hugging him, tickling him and at the same time, feeling his head for fever. After what we'd been through, when the kid cleared his throat I panicked.

But not that year. We were done with all that. Life was good, happy, settled for the first time in years and I was not going to dwell on anything else for another minute. The day before Thanksgiving, Chad still had a runny nose, but he was his normal, engaging self so I shrugged it off.

Thanksgiving morning Chad went out to the curb and performed Broadway show tunes for all the passing cars. He sang, "Putting on the Ritz," imitating Jim Carey in *The Mask.* He was dancing, doing high leg kicks, using a cane and getting beeped by every passing car. By the time our guests had arrived Chad had moved the show inside. Everyone noticed his cold, but no one dwelled on it. We were just so happy to have the day.

The next morning Chad still didn't feel well. I was a little nerved out, but it was black Friday, Don was off work and I didn't want anything to ruin our holiday weekend. By Sunday night I couldn't keep it in any longer. I was angry that Chad couldn't catch so much as a cold without me worrying terribly.

"Don, what do you think? He's had a cold for a week now?"

"It's been concerning me all week, Pen, but since you weren't saying anything I figured I wouldn't either. I was hoping, like you, it would go away on its own and not be an issue."

Panic was back, knocking on the kitchen door.

The next morning I took Chad to the bus stop. Our neighbor, Frank was already there with his kids. He took one look at Chad and asked, “Penny, do you think he’s okay?”

“Yeah, he’s great. Just has a cold.”

“But I thought he couldn’t get sick?”

My heart slid to the ground, bounced around a few times, taking on more than a few bruises before sliding back up to my throat where I practically choked on it.

Who was I kidding? Chad was never a sickly child, not prone to colds or infections. All he ever got was cancer.

I put him on the bus and went home to call Dr. Wasserman.

“Why don’t we wait until Friday, Penny? I’m not on the in patient hospital floor again until then. If the cancer is back, waiting won’t matter. And if it isn’t, waiting a few days will give him a chance to recover from his cold. I called Don at the office and cried. Thereafter followed a week-long series of gambits, playing “Let’s Make a Deal” with God who apparently, from his reaction, wasn’t very fond of game shows.

On Friday morning, Don said he wanted to go to the hospital, but if he went that would mean he had no faith in a clear diagnosis so he was going to work to prove how sure he was that Chad was okay. The hospital visit was strictly routine.

Chad and I left early so we'd have time to run errands, do some shopping and, irony of ironies, even get Chad a haircut. We went to lunch at our favorite Japanese restaurant.

"Okay, baby. We delayed this long enough," I said. "Time to face the music."

Chad was the happiest little boy in the playroom at the clinic that day, chattering away with the other kids. I was a mess. Something was lying in wait for me there. I could feel its hot breath on my ankles, but I couldn't see it, shrouded as it was in Chad's as yet untested blood samples.

When the first results came back, the lab technician told me the numbers were normal. We were still waiting on other numbers, but the initial results were enough for me. I took my first breath in days, called Don and my parents, repeated what the technician had told me. Chad was normal. Life was normal.

Then I saw Dr. Wasserman's face. He was approaching quickly so I hung up the phone.

"Oh please, oh my, is it bad?" My throat had a kilo of dust in it.

"Penny," Dr. Wasserman said, "it appears that the cancer's back."

My legs buckled. "You're kidding right?"

Wrong words. You should have seen him. Like he would kid about something like this. I fell back against the wall and cried at about the same time Chad emerged from the playroom. Dr. Wasserman delivered the news. The first words out of his little seven-year old mouth were:

"Am I going to die?"

"You have a better chance of dying than living," he said. Dr. Wasserman never lied. "Let's get your father up here quick and we'll see what this means."

Chapter 17

Pop Goes the Miracle

I called Don. "It's back. Get here quick."

His office staff later told me he just dropped his instruments and flew out the door. He made record time driving from South Jerseyto Philadelphia, but confessed he didn't remember driving or how he got to CHOP without killing himself or someone else. He walked off the elevator, grabbed Chad the minute he saw him, and squeezed him for all he was worth. To this day Chad remembers that hug; he always said his dad had squeezed the cancer right out of him.

Now it was Don's turn to cry. I clung to him and Chad, my two men, as we headed to a private room where Dr. Wasserman was waiting. He was no longer our doctor. Over the last four years Dr. Wasserman had graduated to close friend and he looked as sad and defeated as we did.

Chad was experiencing a disconnect – he felt fine, healthy, happy – and the diagnosis didn't make sense.

We sat in painful silence for a few moments, catching our collective breath before Dr. Wasserman began. He explained how the cancer's rapid return, less than a year since Chad went off treatment, spelled disaster for a good prognosis with chances of survival going from eighty to five percent and that was only if there was a match. Chad needed a bone marrow transplant, but the donor would have to be a sibling match in order for Chad to have the best chance. Without the transplant he'd likely die. He didn't mince words, just laid it all out for us, and it was tough to hear, but preferable to false hope. Don looked into Dr. Wasserman's eyes and said "take me, please. I'll die for my son, let him live."

Dr. Wasserman just put his hand on Don's shoulder, looking as sad as the rest of us. *Be careful what you wish for.*

"This is my worst nightmare," Chad said to Dr. Wasserman. Please don't let me die. I've been good." *As if goodness meant anything in this world.*

"We have a tripped planned to Disney World in a few weeks," Chad said. "Can I please go there first? Then I'll take care of being sick. I feel fine, I swear."

"Chad, I'm sorry," said Dr. Wasserman. "You can't go to Disney World or anywhere else now. Let's try to help you so hopefully you can go again soon. We'll do everything in our power. You know I'll never lie to you. Trust me to try to make you feel better again."

Dr. Wasserman's choice of words was not lost on me. He may be able to help him feel better, but he had very little faith in helping him survive. Chad went from placid to panic in 0.3 seconds.

The beast had come again, reinforced, unrecognizable; this chimera, this collection of mutant cells had every advantage. Despite all the advances of medical science, we may as well have been fighting a saber-toothed tiger with stakes, stones and spears, hardly a match for such an odds-on favorite. I'd let my son down and everyone else who'd been praying for Chad by failing to hold the miracle.

"Under the circumstances, you can't go home," It was Dr. Wasserman, but he may as well have been transmitting from underwater, so garbled were the sounds my ears were hearing. "There's an experimental protocol, but it's very toxic to the system. Let's see if Faith's bone marrow matched first and if not, we'll discuss our only remaining option."

We knew how horrible this disease was the first time around and here he was, telling us it was going to be a hundred times worse. This time we were more educated, more informed, and so much more afraid. I felt like I was staring into a yawning crevice, a black hole, a superhighway to hell. I remember feeling my legs give out, of being thirsty but unable to drink, of being numb to everything but the scenario before me, playing over and over like the broken record it had become. Don looked beaten, in a state of shock. He had no physical resemblance to the man I'd married.

And like before, a wheelchair appeared magically at our feet, an IV was inserted into Chad's arm and we were escorted upstairs to Seven East, the cancer ward. It was December 1, 1995, exactly one year to the day of Chad finishing his first treatment protocol.

And what about Faith? Who would deliver the devastating news to her, that our lives were going to be turned inside out again? Who would share with her the horror of her new nightmare? My father was elected to greet Faith at the school bus at the end of the day and give her the news. He said Faith burst into tears, asked if Chad was going to die and how long it would be this time that she had to live apart from her mommy. Faith was headed for another period of loneliness and abandonment which I was powerless to prevent.

The next few days blurred by just as they had in October 1991. Chad became sick fast as if Dr. Wasserman's diagnosis had shattered all of our illusions of Chad ever living a normal life. After that, he just gave into it.

He needed so many blood transfusions; he needed surgery to have a central line (a broviac) inserted into his chest since there was no way he'd be able to handle the sheer volume of IV's this time. He needed what seemed like a million chest x-rays. And again with the probing and prodding, as if he was a piece of meat.

Before all this mishigos – craziness – started, I was a champion sleeper, never had any trouble like so many do. But for the next seventeen months, I struggled to keep my eyes closed, waking at the slightest cough or rustle. Sleep deprivation is a form of torture for a reason: it's effective. Sleep, like water or air, is something the body positively cannot live without, yet here I was with barely a wink a night to my credit. It's a wonder I didn't become delusional.

Everything seemed so much worse this time; no one seemed positive. This time, the nurses and docs would look down or over to the side when they spoke to me. This time a team of doctors whom I'd never met would come and examine Chad over and over again. This time all the staff would ever say in response to my questions was, "if we didn't think there was hope we wouldn't try."

Over the next few days, Don, Faith and I were tested to see if our bone marrow matched. Once again, so many of our friends were donating platelets and blood directly to Chad. A man I never met heard of Chad's dilemma and through Idie, my friend, he set up a blood/platelet drive for us. Once again the phone chain and prayer lists were back in service. Once again, Rabbi Krauss was schlepping to Philadelphia via bus and train in order to recite healing prayers over Chad. Once again I went in search of the *similarly situated* in order to gain through strength in numbers; this time all I found were kids in a better place than my baby.

After a few days, Dr. Wasserman gave us the decimating news.

"I'm sorry. None of the bone marrows matched. Chad's chances of survival are even less."

It's a wonder I didn't throw up on his shoes.

"Now what?" Don asked.

"Well," Dr. Wasserman said. "We can go to the bone marrow registry, try to find an unrelated match that may be close, but honestly, it's not going to be a good solution. There's a disease called *Graft v. Host.* If the donor is an unrelated match that doesn't take, the disease becomes so much more severe. I won't lie to you. Most likely Chad is not going to live."

"No, please noooo," I was screaming. "Isn't there anything you can give him? This is CHOP. You're supposed to be the best. If you can't fix him, who can?"

"Penny, I'm sorry. His chances for survival are less than five percent."

"You're wrong, Dr. Wasserman," I said, practically spitting the words out. "So wrong. His chances of survival are one hundred percent. Either he lives or he dies. Please," I begged, "Help him live."

For the next three weeks, the doctors looked for just the right chemo, hoping to put Chad in remission while we signed waiver after waiver and prayed for yet another miracle. They finally came to us with an experimental protocol, extremely high risk, perhaps even more so than the bone marrow transplant from an unrelated match. It was a precise, timed chemo and required his hospitalization for at least an entire year. During that time, he'd receive chemo and then they'd monitor his blood. As soon as the levels hit a certain number they'd hit him again with another round of chemo, and another, and another until the beast had been beaten into submission, bloodied and senseless. The only problem was, as went the beast, so did Chad. He had no recovery time and the side effects were atrocious. He'd be prone to heart failure and comas, would come to rely on breathing machines and pain meds just so he could stay in his body, and whoever stayed with him would be in for a rough time as witness to the melee that no child should have to endure. Since straws were all they were offering, we drew ours. We'd do anything to save Chad, but had run out of choices. We signed on for that crazed procedure and it lasted seventeen months. They could have talked all day and it wouldn't have prepared us for how horrible that year and a half really was. Chad and I moved into our new "residence" on December 1, 1995, and didn't move out until March 1997.

Don and I were wrecks, not eating or sleeping or focusing on much of anything. My mom stayed with me at the hospital because I knew I couldn't do it alone, not this time. So Chad had two people with him at all times: either me and my mom or me and Don. Once again my parents gave up their lives to rescue mine. This disease was destroying our family on so many levels.

Worst of all was watching Chad suffer. It was December 31, 1995, three weeks into the relapse, and Don and I were still stumbling about on autopilot while Chad lay in a coma. The doctors told us that Chad's condition was grave and the next few days critical. He was fighting four types of pneumonia and his lungs were so weak they could give out at any time. On New Year's Eve, 1995, the docs hovered outside Chad's hospital room like some cross-dressing grim reapers. Instead of black robes and scythes they wore lab coats and carried stethoscopes.

"He won't live until midnight," they murmured under their collective breaths. His heart and blood pressure had plummeted to levels barely able to maintain life.

Don and I kept the vigil. And somewhere in that craziness, I fell asleep. If I met the angel of death on the astral plane that night I hope I kicked its sorry-winged butt all the way back to Broad Street. All I know is that the next recollection I had was of someone tugging at my sleeve. I jumped with a start, petrified to hear the next few words.

"Wake up," Dr. Need said. "Chad's taken a turn for the better. I think he's going to survive. His vitals are strong and he's showing signs of coming out of the coma. You might have yourself a miracle here. Happy New Year."

I ran to the playroom and woke Don with the news, then called my parents. Just like that, Abracadabra, before our eyes, Chad started to heal.

It sure seemed that something magical was happening to our son.

Chad did awake that night from his first of many comas that year. He became so weak from the chemo treatments that comas became an almost regular event. He lay there, hooked up to breathing machines, morphine pumps, catheters, and feeding tubes. They looked like dozens of writhing snakes, coiled and squeezing the life out of him which they almost did. He had to learn to walk and talk and even eat and go to the bathroom again such was the devastating toll the chemo took on his muscles. He had weekly bone marrow aspirations as well as lumbar punctures, brain radiation, mouth sores, liver damage, kidney failure, and cardiac arrest. He had what seemed like a bazillion emergency broviac operations due to sepsis, an infection that enters the bloodstream.

The broviac was the central line placed near the nipple through which they administered chemo. It's named for the man who invented it. Chad hated it`. He'd ask the nurse at 5:30 a.m. everyday, "Is it morning? Change my broviac dressing." He was so afraid to see the wires coming out of his body he just wanted it done.

As was typical, Don stepped in and took control where he could, teach Chad to face his fears head on. He taught Chad how to flush the lines clean by himself. What was a team effort became a family affair when Faith signed on as the official time-keeper, making sure the antiseptic was going for a full thirty seconds before continuing with the sterilization procedure. And still through it all we prayed and prayed that God would spare Chad any more suffering.

Chapter 18

No Bed, No Blanket, Go Home

I spent the first of those horrific months in a state of trepidation, so utterly wiped out that even breathing had become a chore. But Chad's near non-existent blood pressure, critically low heart rate and inability to breath on his own kept me vigilant. Night after night I went without rest, running on fumes or adrenaline or just plain fear, I don't know. Finally, Dr. Hammer, bless his well-meaning heart, came to me and said:

"Penny, whether Chad lives or dies won't be because you didn't sleep. You need to go home one night and rest."

"No, I'm not leaving."

"Penny, as one of Chad's doctors, I'm ordering you to leave. You aren't helping the situation by being so exhausted. You're going to get sick yourself and end up an inpatient."

"No, I'm not leaving." As I said before, I can be stubborn or strong-willed when I need to. Later, when I returned from the bathroom I discovered my chair, which also turned into a bed at night, was missing. Saying I'd become territorial was an understatement.

Like a trapper, I followed Dr. Hammer's trail.

"Where's my chair?" I snapped.

"I had it removed. Now there's nowhere for you to sit. Go home, Penny."

"No." I gathered a bunch of blankets and constructed a makeshift bed.

"You can't do this," Dr. Hammer said. "I'm having them removed.

And he did. Right before my eyes. So right in front of his eyes I dumped my suitcase on the floor and put out on my clothes. We may as well have been pissing on each other. Again, he had them removed.

"Penny, am I correct? Don't you have other children at home?"

"Yes," I replied, fuming.

"What good are you to them if you're sick and exhausted? Go home. Have dinner with your family. Sleep in your own bed. Spend time with your daughter. She needs you too. Come back early morning."

He'd hit my nerve center. Neutral territory. *Home!* Time with Faith! What a magnificent concept.

His words were like the proverbial oasis, a shimmering spot of life, a balm for an aching body and soul. Since my sister, Susan was visiting from Colorado, and since my mother encouraged me, I headed for home. Susan subbed in, taking my place as the monitor of Chad's continued existence and my mom picked me up at the hospital. I thought Chad wouldn't even know I was missing. I whispered to him that I'd be back in a few hours, that Aunt Susan would be here in case he woke up and that I was just a phone call away and I'd come right back if he woke up. Then I left.

Big Mistake. We'd only made it to the Walt Whitman Bridge when my beeper went off. It was Dr. Hammer so I drove off the closest exit and called him back so petrified on what he might tell me.

"Penny," Dr. Hammer said. "Get here quick. Chad just went code blue. As we turned the car around and headed back into the city, I watched the sands shift and roll, swallowing up all that shimmering blue water. The oasis proved to be a mirage.

We raced back to the hospital and in my head I talked to Chad the whole time, telling him to hang on, that Mommy was coming. I think he must have heard me because when I got there they were all surrounding him, his doctors and nurses and med techs. His heartbeat was erratic, but he was stable.

I grabbed his hand. "Baby, Mommy's back." His blood pressure responded immediately. And before I could say a word, Dr. Hammer apologized.

"I'm sorry. I was wrong. You win. Chad needs you. Please don't leave again."

I just took Dr. Hammer's hand and cried.

Chapter 19

One Prescription for Time, Please

How much toxicity could one little body take? The chemo brought on so many comas and again, as we'd done before, we called on Rabbi Krauss to come to Philadelphia and say the Mishaberach – a prayer for the seriously ill and often times dying – over Chad. When he got to CHOP, Rabbi Krauss whispered something to Chad as he lay there and then aloud, in a deep strong voice, like Moses parting the Red Sea said,

"Chad, listen to me. Open your eyes and look at your mother. Look at that face. If you could do as I ask you would see the saddest Mommy in the world. Don't do this to your mother, Chad. It's not time. Open your eyes." Jews use that ever powerful tool, guilt, even in life and death situations. Rabbi Krauss was guilting Chad into living and using me as the bait. Had I thought about it at the time I would have laughed. But hey, I'd take his continued living however I could get it.

Then Rabbi Krauss continued, but this time less like Moses and more like Billy Crystal: "If you do, I promise you the biggest best party of your life. We'll have a huge celebration, but you have to wake up so we can do it." Nothing happened. Even Moses seemed to have better response time. After a while, Rabbi Krauss left.

Seven days later Chad emerged from his coma. My mother, Don and I were keeping the vigil as he stirred. We leaped up and surrounded the bed as he opened his eyes for the first time in what felt like forever. Chad's first words were: "Did he have the party without me?"

I leaned in close and said, "What? Hi, baby, welcome back," crying all over him.

"Did he have the party without me?" Chad repeated. "Did I miss my own party?"

Oh my God, Chad had heard him; he'd heard the Rabbi's promise and that gave him strength to live.

Years later, the Rabbi made good on his promise but not before years of horror, pain, loss and lots of magic. To this day, Chad loves a good party.

In March1996 when Chad was at his worst, in so much physical danger and so much pain that even five percent chance of survival seemed unimaginable, the doctors came to me and said, "Mrs. Juros, we're going to move Chad to intensive care. That way he'll have a one on one nurse and 24/7 care. Plus they're better equipped to help him with his pain. We'll intubate him which means will give him a needle that will put him in a very deep sleep. He won't feel any pain and he won't have to push for the morphine pump. He'll rest more."

It should have sounded like a good idea; Chad was in excruciating pain and this would have relieved it. But something wasn't right. I called Don, crying, even though at the time I didn't realize what was happening: they were preparing Chad for death.

Don left work to keep watch with me in ICU to mourn and grieve with me in the way we dealt with all aspects of our lives – together. I rarely left Chad alone, but since Don was there, I went to the cafeteria to get something to eat. On my way back to the ICU, two doctors boarded the elevator and from my spot in the back, I heard one say,

"We've got seven very sick children today, but none is as bad as that little magic boy. He probably won't live until midnight. It's such a shame."

"Excuse me," I said my voice timid and unsteady. "Excuse me, are you speaking about my son, Chad

Juros. Is he the magic boy who won't make it to midnight?"

Oh, the looks on their faces. Caught discussing a patient in the elevator, a grave infraction, but worse, their words! What a way to deliver a bombshell.

"Mrs. Juros, if I could give you anything in life my prescription to you and your son would be time."

He handed me a prescription with a date and time and his signature on it and real big in the middle of the paper it said: TIME. He couldn't meet my eyes when he handed it to me. The elevators doors opened and I was alone. I sunk to the floor.

Years later, I said the same thing to others in pain. Time, a fourth-dimension, non-linear, intangible and unquantifiable concept is really all we have. Go figure. You'll find you can't.

Weeks later, after much of the same treatment and reactions, the doctors suggested we have the Rabbi come and do any final blessings over Chad. His blood pressure had dropped so low that they expected him to have a stroke or die soon. I called Don who was at the tennis courts – his one release from all the pressure and pain. Don raced to the hospital to be with us. He arrived an hour later all sweaty and smelly, still wearing his tennis garb. He approached the bed where I was hovering over Chad and whispered something in his son's ear. Within seconds, Chad's blood pressure had spiked.

The nurse jumped up and said, "Dr. Juros, what did you say? Say it again." Don bent over and whispered again to Chad and again Chad's blood pressure spiked. So Don whispered over and over again while the nurse got the doctor who came running in and checked Chad's vitals.

"Whatever you're saying, Dr. Juros, keep talking. He's responding."

Again, my son was back from the brink.

I never did ask Don what he said that day.

Chapter 20

Who's Up for a Little Vacation?

In February 1996, when Faith was turning eleven, she asked for a birthday party at a pizza place with her brother performing the magic. Now, we hadn't left the hospital since we arrived on December 1, 1995 so her request was a bit problematic. But we didn't want to disappoint her, she had enough of that, so I asked Chad's doctors. My request was met with a resounding and emphatic shake of the head. Because of the need to flush the chemo it just wasn't possible. Faith was really disappointed.

But then Ruth, Chad's nurse practitioner had a brilliant idea. She suggested Chad have his regular treatment on Friday and be discharged with two treatments that Don, as a doctor, could administer. This particular chemo wasn't highly toxic; Don could be trained. The docs weren't thrilled, but acquiesced. In addition to the boxes of saline solution we'd need, Chad was fitted for a backpack which was hooked to his tubes and wires and broviac. Don would have to continually check that the chemo was being flushed through is system. If it failed or something went wrong, we'd have to bring Chad right back. The four of us thought we'd won the lottery. We were going home for the weekend.

Word spread. Chad's friend's parents organized a bowling party. We went right there from the hospital; Chad was thrilled. He was weak, walking with a limp, weighed down by his backpack and bald as a bowling ball, but he could care less. He was just so happy to play with his friends. We had three lanes and pizza and one of the best nights ever, pretending to be normal.

The next day was all for Faith. About sixty friends and family crowded into this small pizza shop to celebrate her birthday. Chad gave a flawless fifteen-minute performance before introducing *The Great Donaldo.* I donned my cheerleader face and tried to look unconcerned, but my stomach was churning; I was terrified.

That night I wanted Chad to rest, but he wanted to play. So more friends came over to watch movies and hang out. Don and I huddled together, watching our emotions run circles around us. We were beat, physically and mentally, and although the kids slept great, Don and I had a worrisome repose. The next morning we went out for breakfast then back to the hospital. Maybe we really didn't want the mini-vacation after all, stressful as it was. Even Chad was pooped.

And although I hadn't admitted it to myself at the time, I noticed a slight change in Don, not a lot of bounce to his step or bubble to his personality. I told myself he'd have his breakdown, Chad would survive, and eventually, all would be well. What the hell did I know?

Chapter 21

Presenting Our New Normal

Life at the hospital developed a patina of normalcy, making it just palatable enough to be tolerated. Chad was the first child to ever have lived so long as a result of this protocol. They were looking to him on what to do with the next patient. If Chad went into cardiac arrest, they knew what to tweak in the chemos for the next child. Life as a guinea pig didn't pay well, but our son was still alive and that's what we were counting on.

Through all this, my husband and I were mainly communicating by phone. I'd witnessed so many marriages fall apart from the stress of this disease, but Don and I stayed solid. He'd call me after he got to work in the morning and always spoke with Chad even when he was in a coma not knowing what Chad might be able to hear. I'd fill him in on the details of our night and he'd go back to his patients. At lunch, he'd call me again and then once more in the afternoon. We'd be in touch constantly in the evening.

But while life became routine for Chad and I, it was anything but for Faith and Don. My parents move helped tremendously. They still worked, from 4 a.m. to 12 p.m., so they could get Faith off the bus and give her dinner. But the weird hours necessitated weird sleeping arrangements in order for Faith to get back to school in the morning. We coped as humans always do when circumstances called.

On Monday nights, Faith would routinely sleep at her friend, Rachel's. On Tuesday nights, I would go home and clean my house, do payroll for the office, do laundry, grocery shop, lay out Faith's clothes and make her lunches for the week, have dinner with her and sleep with her in my bed. I'd tell her over and over how special she was, that I didn't pick one child over the other and that if I had any magical powers at all, I'd make it so we were home together as a family each night. The last thing I wanted her to feel was abandonment. And in those quiet times she'd catch me up on what her normal routine was like. I loved those moments despite the dread that periodically crept into my consciousness and perched on a balcony in my frontal lobes, waiting for my attention to drift enough to catch me unaware, pounce and depart, leaving its oily footprints for me to follow. *What if he were queasy? What if he couldn't eat? What if they gave him the wrong meds? How was Don holding up?*

One time I caught the nurse giving Chad medication for a boy named Chaz and since then I became a control freak, watching every tube insertion, having Don call me every time someone entered the room that wasn't there simply to check vitals, and even then I wanted to know the temperature readings, blood counts, and Chad's general mood. It would have been easier on everyone had I just stayed at the hospital – everyone but Faith, that is. I needed to spend at least this bit of time with my baby girl, and Chad needed to be with his father.

And so it went. Wednesday nights Don picked Faith up at the bus and they'd sleep at home. On Thursday nights she went to my parents. On weekends she went anywhere and everywhere with whoever would have her which is why she's so independent today.

Since cell phones weren't popular yet, I raised Faith by beeper. She'd beep me in the morning before she left for school. I'd call her back and offer fashion advice, tell her to have a nice day. She'd beep me as soon as she got off the bus and tell me about tests and homework and projects and assemblies.

I missed every single assembly from kindergarten through 7th grade because they always seemed to be on days Chad had a bone marrow aspiration or a spinal or when he was in a coma and too sick for me to leave. I'd send my parents in my place – as if anyone could replace a mother – while my heart ached for her. I told her again and again how I wished I didn't have to make those choices. I started her in grief counseling for even though I wasn't dead to her, at times I may as well have been. The therapist said she always drew pictures of fire and destruction.

Years later, a "friend" told me that now things had settled down she didn't feel bad telling me that on one of the weekends I was at the hospital she had taken Faith with her to the movies and for a slice of pizza. I thanked her.

"Oh, no problem, Penny. I was thrilled to help out, do my part. By the way, you owe me nine dollars, including tip."

I almost died. I gave her ten and told her to keep the change.

Could I have done better by my daughter? In retrospect, perhaps, although even now, it's hard to see what I could have done differently. As a mother, my instinct, no matter how contrary to the rules in the animal kingdom, was to help the weakest one. I wish it didn't seem like I was always dumping Faith off somewhere, but that's a pretty accurate description of those years. Thankfully, and with the help of so many friends and loved ones – and several beepers – that child of mine, my first born, found her way through some very real fires of hell and emerged, maybe not unscathed, but fired to a shimmery luster, to become the wonderful woman she is today: strong, capable, independent.

Faith's represents normalcy in my life. She represents stability. She's my hero.

Chapter 22

Presenting, The Magical Chadakazam

Don's erratic behavior was getting worse. Faith would call me at the hospital.

"Mommy, Daddy's doing it again," she'd say.

"What Faith? What's Daddy doing?"

"He told me he was confused on where we live. He said he got lost driving home from work"

"Huh? How could that be?" We basically live on a straight line from his office to our house.

"I know, Mommy. He's acting weird like he did last summer when Chad was better."

Another word about my amazing daughter who, like her brother was forced to grow up too quickly. She was no longer afraid of the hospital and when Chad relapsed, she came regularly. But while Chad was trying to survive there, she was trying to survive at home with her father. Don had appeared to be depressed, lethargic and self-isolating. He saw doctors complaining of frozen shoulder and joint pain, hand weakness, lack of energy and appetite only to be repeatedly told it was depression.

"Who can blame you? You and your wife are living separate lives, struggling to save your son's life while still running your dental practice and trying to be both mother and father to your daughter. It makes sense. It's depression." Again and again, the same diagnosis.

But it wasn't depression and while I had not a spare ounce of time or energy to deal with it logically, my daughter, my strong and independent little girl was left with the unpleasant repercussions. How brave and big of her.

So I'd speak to Don and he'd always seem shocked to hear he did the things Faith said he was doing since he didn't remember doing them.

"Are you tired?" I'd ask.

"No," he'd say.

"Depressed?"

"No."

After one of these incidents Don would have a period of time where life seemed good again. Then out of the blue his receptionist would call me and say, "Penny is your husband okay? He's sitting in the dark in his office, barely moving. He told me not to cancel his patients, but when someone cancels he told me not to fill the slot. He'd rather rest. But the accounts receivable are going way down."

I'd sit there monitoring Chad's wires, tubes and beepers and worry about Don. *Was he crumbling? Showing signs of a nervous breakdown?*

It had to be harder on the extended family than on Chad and I. Our lives weren't in our control. We did what we were told. Chad laid there and slept or watched a movie, perfected a magic trick or played in the playroom, but whatever he did he was in the best possible hands in the world. And I felt safer being there than at home. The outside world could only guess what was happening. People would call me distraught, expecting the worst and I'd be perky. I really had no good news to report, but I realized it wasn't what I said, but how I said it. I became everyone's cheerleader.

"Hi, how are you?" I'd say in my sing-song happy voice. "Chad's resting now." The truth was he was in a coma in critical condition, but he *was* resting and not dead so he was doing well. Hey, everyone handled their stress differently. I happened to use humor, even when I was the only one in on the joke.

Lucky for me I had at least one friend for whom I didn't need to wave the pom poms – my friend Ivy – a friend who'd feed me jokes. When things were bleak and Chad was always on the verge of dying, at 10:20 a.m. everyday, the phone would ring, faithfully as the rising sun. Her children were the same age as mine, and like me, she was a worry wart. She'd gossip for a few minutes in an attempt to make me feel normal about life and then ask for the update. When I'd share that if nothing else, he's still alive, she'd say "keniherra, poo poo poo" which translates to "thank God" or "God forbid," or something like that, and is the Jewish way to chase away the bad luck. For seventeen months straight she did this, telling me jokes, making me laugh. She was an integral part of my surviving that wretched time.

As was Don for Chad. To Chad, I was the nurturer, but Daddy was the fun one. Daddy had the laughs. Daddy had the magic. Even when Don was deteriorating from the inside out, behaving erratically at work, broken to the rest of the world, to Chad he was fun and fluid and vigorous. He never let Chad see him down, not when Chad was sick. Chad always saw his inner glow, even as it was dimming.

"Pen, it hit me," Don said. "This is Chad's life. Even if he's an inpatient in ICU, it's his childhood and if we let it go by without doing something special it will only be remembered as cancer. Cancer can't be his childhood. And since I can't be his Little League coach and I can't teach him tennis as I did with Faith, I need to find something I can do with him while he's lying in a hospital bed. I was thinking of ideas, something that just he and I can bond with."

Well, both guys loved *Star Trek* and making movies and building rockets, but more than anything, my two guys loved magic. And since they were already dabbling at the forefront, Don decided to go into the attic and pull out all the magic props he had as a child, really throw himself into teaching Chad the craft.

Soon the only movies playing in Chad's room were ones that taught magic. Soon the only books that Chad read were magic books. And every single Tuesday, bar none, Don would bring Chad one more trick to learn. He wanted Chad to perfect the trick, master the skill before he moved on to another. Magic became the dominant theme in Chad's life; everyone knew about this sick little magical boy and his magical father. Magic became Chad's focus, his reason for living. We learned that, ironically, the word Abracadabra derives from a Hebrew word that is defined as "a magic word, the letters of which were arranged in an inverted pyramid and worn as An amulet around the neck to protect the wearer against disease or trouble. One fewer letter appeared in each line of the pyramid, until only *a* remained to form the vertex of the triangle. As the letters disappeared, so supposedly did the disease or trouble."

Word spread and after awhile, the life specialists came to me and asked if Chad was ready to perhaps perform a little magic show in the playroom. I deferred to Don who requested a week or so to perfect a routine with Chad. In the interim, Don went out and bought Chad an outfit complete with top hat and cape. He even brought the video camera to tape Chad's performance so they could watch it later and critique it like Monday morning game tapes.

The play therapist was wheeling in patients from all over the ward, and with the nurses and docs, the place was packed. Don rolled out the music and Chad began his first routine. And that day in his first ever public performance, Chad was bitten by the magic bug. He was seven, and he's been obsessed ever since.

Chapter 23

I'll Be There

Several more months passed and Chad was finally tolerating the chemo's well enough that the docs said we could go home between regimens. Yet another new normal began. Chad and I would be admitted on Friday after visiting with Dr. Wasserman in the clinic and would stay until the following Wednesday. Barring any horrible reactions or fever spikes, we'd check out Wednesday night and would sometimes stay home for up to three weeks with three visits per week to the local hospital to check Chad's blood counts interspersed for good measure.

But home care had its down sides. There was chemo to administer, tubes and packs and wires to clean and account for, all the worries and concerns of the hospital sans the amazing team of doctors and nurses and round-the-clock care. It took its toll on Don and me even though being at home allowed us to escape the perpetual sadness of that hospital setting.

The oncology unit at the hospital was like a war zone, its halls littered with the splintered remains of dead and dying children. The parents and children inhabiting Seven East were living their own private holocaust; pain, horror and mass destruction were everywhere. Over the seventeen months that Chad was an inpatient, twenty-two of his roommates died before our eyes. We'd go to bed with them at night and by morning they'd be gone. I had people break down screaming at me because Chad was living while their children were dying. I knew two mothers who jumped off the Walt Whitman Bridge when their children relapsed. In one case, the child lived. Chad used to ask me what color crayon his roommates were. He noticed that so many, including himself, were either orange, yellow or sometimes green from being jaundiced when their livers weren't functioning or from puking, etc. Each morning he'd ask me "what color crayon am I today, Mom?"

One evening when everyone was asleep and all was quiet in the halls, I went to the doorway, my hang out spot, and noticed the lights flicker. I realized that everyone else's door was closed. From down the hall I saw my friend come out of her room, holding onto the gurney as if she'd never let it go. Next to her was her daughter, Chad's friend, Lisa, her face covered with a sheet. I can't even describe my emotions at that moment. I didn't know how to react when they passed by, hadn't even known that Lisa had taken a turn for the worst. No wonder they'd shut the doors and lights. The next morning, I heard that three children had died during the night.

One of the saddest things to witness was the kids who were left at CHOP without any parent, guardian or caretaker. One child was actually dropped off by a cab with a change of clothes in a plastic bag and a note saying, "when's he's better, have a cab drop him off at this address."

I used to sit and rock those children, the ones with no one, bring them food and toys, just hug them so they didn't feel they were alone in the world. When Chad was stable he would say to me, "I'm okay now, Mom. Go hug *so and so*, he could really use a warm touch." I'm not sure who those hugs did more for, me or them.

While in the hospital, I attended weekly grief therapy sessions, but they left me more depressed than when I'd walked in. The stories were incredible, some amazing miracles, some horrible failures, and always tales of mourning and loss. I felt guilty that Chad was doing so well. Why our son was surviving when the doctors told us he was sicker than those other children was a mystery to us. But eventually we developed a "who cares" attitude. Who cares why as long as he is? We'd take it any way we could get it. I noticed other parents, parents of children not doing as well as Chad, avoiding me. Still others sought me out for support and comfort. I was a two-timer, my son a survivor. Just about anything that was happening to their children I'd experienced, waded through and come up on the opposite shore. I was something to be analyzed, questioned and studied.

When Chad was first diagnosed with leukemia, I called the Principal of Chad's private school and asked him – he happened to be a pediatrician – to please educate Chad's teachers and the staff at Hebrew Academy.

Dr. Kesslerman replied, "Penny, it's going to feel to you that Chad and you are climbing the highest mountain and just when you reach the top there'll be another mountain and another and another. And you'll be hoping, praying for it to end or just to clear the next hurdle, but there will always be one more mountain. But one day, when you're so beaten and Chad is so exhausted and you both feel like you can't go another step then all of a sudden you'll get to the top of the next mountain and when you turn and look to your future you'll see an anthill."

It was years and years before we got to that anthill, and for a good long time I wasn't even sure if it was real, or just another mirage.

One night when we were in our on again off again home routine, Chad came to me and said as he did many times, "I want to lay with you." He snuggled in and I wrapped my arms around him.

I was reading, *Why Bad Things Happen to Good People* at the time and after scanning the title he asked, "All I want to know is why did I have to get *mekemia* (as he pronounced it for years) a second time? What went wrong?"

"No one knows Chad, but this book tells you that we shouldn't ask the whys because it doesn't matter. It talks about what we can do to go on from here."

"Well, I want to know why there are so many sicker kids out there. People should pray for them."

"Everyone loves you, Chad. That's why they pray for you."

"Well, I pray for the other sick kids at the hospital."

"And that's what keeps your father and me going. How you care for others."

It's amazing, isn't it? How much compassion resides in each one of us? Here was this child having a staring contest with death almost routinely, and praying, not for him, but for the other kids. Pop went my heart, exploding past my confining chest area – growing again.

And so were other people. When Chad was first diagnosed my Uncle Mel and Aunt Valerie would call me several times a week asking what they could do to help. "Nothing," I'd reply. "Just hope and pray."

But that wasn't enough for Uncle Mel and Aunt Valerie. Instead they joined Team in Training through the National Lymphoma and Leukemia Society and walked in marathons across the world in Chad's name. They'd never done anything like that before yet here they were, walking in Alaska, Florida, Washington, Phoenix and Atlantic City, carrying pictures, displaying Chad's name on their chests, raising funds and public awareness in the search for the cure. Years later when Chad was strong and healthy enough to travel, he'd meet them at the finish line, cheering for them the way they'd cheered for him all those times. But it wasn't just Uncle Mel and Aunt Valerie. There were so many people, and they were always there for us.

In 1991, when Chad was first diagnosed with leukemia, one of the songs on the charts was the remake of Michael Jackson's *I'll Be There.*

You and I must make a pact.
We will bring salvation back.
Where there is love.
I'll be there.

I'll reach out my hand, to you.
I'll have faith, in all you do.
Just call my name.
I'll be there.

I used to sing it to him constantly. It became *our song*. To this day, when I hear that song the memories of that sad time come, all tangled up with the pain and love and anxiety, pouring in and filling me up like flood waters. And because the love is so inextricably interwoven with the pain, I would not trade a single one of those memories for all the money in the world.

Chapter 24

The Day We Never Thought Would Finally Arrived

After so many rounds of chemo, the docs came to Don and me and said they were ready to start brain radiation on Chad, a prophylactic maneuver. Chemotherapy didn't work on the brain or the testes and on the outside chance the cancer was hiding in one of these places; the radiation would assure annihilation of any rebel leukemia cells. They would give him the minimum, five days in a row for three weeks. The problem was the possibility of him developing secondary cancers. Don and I ultimately decided that we could only deal with one cancer at a time, thank you very much, and approved the radiation.

Chad tolerated it like everything else, with a positive attitude. Finally on January 5, 1998, the experimental protocol that Chad began on December 1, 1995 was over. His only requirement was that he visits the hospital once a month for a check up. Dr. Hammer, the same man who tried to take my bed away, took over for Dr. Wasserman after he left to do leukemia research. It had been hard on him, too, and time to move on, he said. Chad enjoyed Dr. Hammer as much as Dr Wasserman who remains, to this day, a dear friend.

I used to go to sleep at night, my pounding heart full of fear and confusion, my head full of useless cancer-related facts. I'd tell Don that I was afraid to close my eyes for fear of what I'd wake up to. Things got so bad with Chad that I started loving sleep again; my nightmares had become more appealing than my reality.

But then I learned something. I learned about the power of the committed collective, and how that group, no matter how small or large, has the power to change the world. There were so many people in our lives during those crucial times: doctors, nurses, volunteers, parents, grandparents, friends, relatives, rabbis, teachers, neighbors, even other patients, pulling for Chad, pulling for us. They brought us toys, greetings, food, prayers and good cheer. They sent gifts of hope, gifts of courage, gifts of wisdom and gifts of faith. They gave of their time and their lives, of their faiths and quite literally their blood. The cancer was a hurdle for us to jump, one that required a cheering section and home court advantage. All those people gave this to us. This large, raucous, unwieldy bunch, some blood, some brothers, now all considered friends, it's their blood running through Chad's veins, and he's alive today because of them all.

If I lived a thousand lifetimes, I couldn't repay all their kindnesses.

PART TWO

Chapter 25

Why I Hate My Birthday More Than Ever

I'd like to say we started 1998 full of hope. Chad's blood was cancer free and there we were, nearing the finish line, closing in on normal. But it wasn't anywhere near normal as we were soon about to discover.

The first part of the year was wonderful. Chad was healthy, we were all living under the same roof and twelve-year old Faith was about to undergo a life-changing event. On Memorial Day 1998 she would become a bat mitzvah.

Friends and family from around the globe were coming. Understand: bat and bar mitzvah's are a major event in the Jewish tradition. A daughter becomes a woman. A son becomes a man. Preparations are discussed years in advance. The synagogue generally gives you the date for your son or daughters event at least a year in advance. And all those years of Hebrew school prepare the bat or bar mitzvah for the traditional ritual reading from the Torah and Haftorah portion. Faith chose to do a mitzvah (good) deed by donating a portion of her gifts to a foundation that funds research for leukemia at CHOP.

Like I said, it's an HUGE big deal.

Faith loves Broadway shows and acting so the theme for her bat mitzvah was Broadway. Playbills from different Broadway musicals became the centerpieces for each of the tables; seating cards were candy bars that looked like tickets to a Broadway show; themes from different musicals were playing throughout the day. It was a blast to plan and everyone remarked how happy we seemed as a family. They did note how thin Don looked, and how distant he seemed. He danced and socialized, but he also seemed a bit peculiar.

But nothing was going to stop me from having the time of my life to date so I shoved my worries under the linen table cloth and just enjoyed the weekend. Friday evening we had the out-of-town guests meet for Chinese food, Saturday was the religious service at the synagogue followed by a reception of dancing, eating, laughing and picture-taking that lasted until early evening. Afterwards we changed our clothes and went to the boardwalk to officially kick off summer.

The next day we had a huge BBQ at our house and finally, Sunday night, everyone went home. It was the last time everyone in our house was ostensibly healthy, and I have the videos to prove it. Shortly thereafter our brief happy, healthy period was over.

On October 21, 1998, my 41st birthday, exactly seven years to the date of Chad's initial diagnosis, and only ten months since Chad had finished his treatments for the second time, Don walked in the door and collapsed in my arms, an inert mass, lying right at my feet. In retrospect, it's a wonder I wasn't reduced to hysterics at that point, given all that our family had suffered in the last seven years, but every cell in my body had been bracing for some mishap, some fumble, some "Do Not Pass Go, Do Not Collect $200." I just wasn't prepared for the size and shape of it, the weight as it pulled me down, the reverberation as we hit the floor.

Had anyone told me in that moment that Don, my husband, my lover, my best friend, my proverbial rock had a single year to live I would have visited with Hysteria big time. But thank God He doesn't tell us what we constantly beg to know. Otherwise, how would any one of us put even a toe on the cold hard floor in the morning?

And so it had begun again. After years of schlepping with Don to doctors with his complaints of numbness in his hands, frozen shoulder, inability to concentrate, and general fatigue, of getting second, third and even fourth opinions, all was about to be revealed.

Dr. Marc Felmer, Don's friend and tennis partner had diagnosed Don just three days before with carpal tunnel syndrome, a diagnosis we could live with. It made sense due to the fact that Don was a dentist. Dr. Felmer scheduled Don for surgery in two days. Two nights before, I spoke with Dr. Wasserman. I was explaining to him my new worry and he asked me to please have Don obtain an MRI before we go ahead with the carpal tunnel surgery. He asked that I get one more opinion. The next day, after a brief exam, Dr. Stackhouse changed our minds. He felt it wasn't classic carpal tunnel and wanted Don to get an MRI from top to bottom. I called Marc when we got home from seeing Dr. Stackhouse and he agreed to cancel the surgery.

The following day, my birthday (God, how I hate that day), Don took the kids to buy me a present. When they got home, he walked in the door and collapsed. I actually caught him. He really didn't fall to the floor, but my brain's memory of the experience, as a clinical third-party observer, makes me perceive it that way. I'm not sure how I managed to get him to the car – my husband wasn't a particularly big guy, but he was very strong and well built – or why I didn't call an ambulance. It was like somebody else took over; replacing me with an entity that could handle what was coming. When we arrived at the hospital, I demanded a total MRI.

"Don, you don't need an MRI. You have carpal tunnel. We'll fix your hand and your head will get better," Marc's associate, Dr. Gelberman said. "Your wife's being a pain in the ass."

"It's my brain and if my wife wants an MRI from head to toe than you do it," Don said. "And don't you ever call her a pain in the ass again."

It took Don collapsing for them to finally do this MRI, but at least we were getting it. I thought for sure they were going to tell us he had epilepsy.

Two hours later, Dr. Gelberman called me at home and said, "Get Don to the hospital fast. And don't let him drive."

I yelled for Don to get ready to go back to Shore Memorial Hospital, about ten minutes from our house. He was actually feeling better – they'd given him Prozac to help with the feeling depressed – and he exercised for the first time in weeks so he didn't feel the sense of urgency that I did, but he complied. My father came over to watch the kids and my mom met us at the hospital.

Once there, they put Don in a holding area in a bed and asked him how he felt about every ten minutes. We were baffled, unsure as to what was happening. Then Marc joined us right from the racquetball court, drenched in sweat, a look of concern on his face.

"What's up? Why all the commotion?" Don asked.

"It seems as though you have a brain tumor. It's called glioblastoma multiforme iv. We'll biopsy it and let you know the prognosis and plan of action," Marc said. His delivery seemed pretty confident which is probably why it didn't feel like someone set off dynamite behind my eyes. Until I saw Marc's colleague, Dr. Gelberman, come in, looking grim, and making no eye contact. *Uh oh.* I knew those signals all too well.

"This is fixable, right?" Marc asked. "They remove the tumor, or shrink it down to nothing and life goes on, right?"

Dr. Gelberman shook her head no and walked away with Marc. Instinctually, of course, I knew what was about to happen, and so did Don. How could we not after the last seven years? But we wanted to shroud ourselves in our cloak of denial for as long as possible, so we stayed there, the two of us, pish poshing on our own private island for the entire fifteen minutes it took Marc to come back and tell us that the island was, in fact, surrounded by salt water and there were no fresh drinking water sources available. In other words, time was running out. He had tears in his eyes and asked to speak to me alone.

Out in the hall, Marc told me Don had brain cancer, that there was no hope or cure, and that Don was scheduled for emergency brain surgery in the morning. He said he was sorry, being wrong about his initial prognosis – as if that would have changed the outcome – sorry about the whole thing.

At the time my initial reaction was to rage, against him, against all the docs who'd seen or treated Don over the last few years, against God and the universe and anyone else who'd happened along my path. Were it not for the shock symptoms which had begun to take effect, the weak knees, the dry cotton-mouth, the muddled thinking processes, perhaps I would have. We want our doctors to deliver a one hundred percent accurate diagnosis every time, to always get it right, to always have a cure. The truth is that sometimes even God struggles in these categories so why not mere mortals who simply have a bit more education than the rest of us. Still, I couldn't help but feel let down, cheated again somehow.

I don't really remember what I said to him, probably just stared in stunned silence. At least with Chad we'd had some chance, albeit small, but a chance all the same. With Don they were offering nothing but death as an option, not my first choice. *How could this be happening again? To my family? My husband? My kids? All over again? To me?* It was hard enough to endure when there was hope....

Things happened pretty quickly after that. They asked if I had a living will and power of attorney for Don. Of course, we didn't. They told me they would draw up papers and have someone come over and sign them immediately. Don couldn't even write his name on the line; he didn't have the strength to hold a pen. The prognosis and seizures had wiped him out. He made an X on the line.

When I told my mother her head hit the wall – literally. She held fast to her son-in-law, repeatedly kissing his cheek. The turmoil had begun.

Chapter 26

Not What You Know But Who You Know

I called Chad's doctors at CHOP because now, after eight years of treating Chad, they were my friends. Dr. Wasserman arranged for Don to be operated on by one of the best neurosurgeons in the world, a highly reputable doctor who was affiliated with Hospital of the University Of Pennsylvania (HUP). HUP arranged for Don to be transported to their hospital immediately and the next morning Don was first on Dr. June's list for emergency brain surgery. Someone else got bumped from the coveted first slot because in life it's never about what you know, but always about who you know. Chad's doctors were influential enough to arrange for Don to be treated stat. I always wondered about the patient who got bumped. Did it matter to them in the long run? It sure didn't change our situation.

Nine hours later Don awoke from surgery. They had debulked the entire tumor, but the doctor explained to us that all that did was buy him some pressure release, not time. The next day there was a family meeting, just as they had done for Chad twice before. The doctors told us that the frozen section of the biopsy seemed to prove their original diagnosis of glioblastoma multiforme IV. Don would be dead most likely within a year.

"Sell your office immediately, make your memories with your children now," they said. "There's no hope and no cure. Don't go searching for that magic bullet like you did for Chad. We have nothing to offer you and you will only be using up your life insurance and reducing your quality of life."

The first words out of Don's mouth were "Poor Penny."

"Poor Penny? Did you hear what Dr. June just said? He said you were going to be dead in less than a year. Why poor Penny?"

Don took my hand: "Pen, I've had everything I ever wanted in life. You, the kids, my office, tennis. You're the one who'll be left alone, trying to figure it out. You put your formal education on hold to put me through dental school and now you'll have to be the breadwinner. A single parent to two children one of which has had cancer twice. I'll be dead, yes, but I'll have died happy because I had you."

I started to cry, a heaving, disconsolate weeping, because I realized, once again, how incredibly unselfish my husband was. When I finally caught my breath, the first thing I said was, "What do we tell the children? No one's moving until we decide. We've got to be honest with them, just like we were with Chad's diagnosis." Everyone agreed.

We decided to tell them that, like Chad, now it was Dad's time to be sick and that we didn't know how long it would take and what the treatments would be like. Then I started begging for at least an attempt to save Don's life. Dr. June suggested NYU, that they had an experimental protocol. It definitely wouldn't buy us a cure, but maybe time. But time in itself could be the magic bullet. If he held on long enough a cure might be discovered.

"You have the strength and capacity to maybe be the miracle," Dr. June said. "You were diagnosed at a young age and your organs are strong because you eat well, you've never smoked and you're a tennis champion."

Let the games begin – again.

Chapter 27

HAPPY 40TH.

One month after his diagnosis, Don turned forty. He came to me about a week before his birthday and asked if we could throw a party. I was shocked. Don, the quiet, unpretentious, private man I married would never had wanted a fuss made over him or his birthday, but this time it was different. This time he knew it was likely his last birthday and he wanted to celebrate big. Laura, being my best friend and the consummate host, offered to have the party at her house. Since Don wanted Chinese food, she created a Chinese theme, inviting everyone by phone quickly. Over a hundred friends and family members showed. Throughout the party, Don sat in a high-backed chair in the corner and everyone approached him individually, like Marlon Brando in *The Godfather*, for some private time and talk. Every time I looked at him he was either crying or laughing over some memory or photo someone brought to share. It was a bittersweet night for us filled with love and laughter and hope and good wishes. Don left his party a very happy man.

Two months and one successful surgery later, we got a glimpse of Don's MRI. There was a gaping hole where the tumor used to be. I couldn't help myself.

"Hey, Dr. Dentist, bet you've never been so thrilled to see a cavity."

Don laughed, but it was short-lived. He was undergoing regular chemotherapy treatments and they were making him sick for days at a time. At the same time, Chad had hives and I just had to ask myself, "whazup with that?" I thought I was cracking up, but then I knew that not to be true. Rather, the world under me was fracturing. My rock was splintering into a thousand billion pieces even as I lay upon it, clinging to its hard smooth surfaces, watching as wind and weather caressed and beat upon it, coaxing and cajoling my fine, strong man with his robust, athletic build, his chiseled jaw, his abdomen like granite.
I watched as he eroded one sinewy muscle at a time, spiraling off into oblivion where skin turned pallid and muscle fell away from bone, lax and shrunken, suspended only by the flesh surrounding it. I feared I would wake to a mound of ash and hair and teeth grown cold in my bed, not my husband, watching while the wind from the open window would have

its way with him. . Was that my religion or someone else's? Do I even know where God is anymore? Or He I?

It's all so absurd. Maybe I've already died and this is some perverse *Ground Hog's Day* type of hell – same crap, different day. My friend Idie checked in, delivered good wishes in tidy little packages, told me she didn't think God specifically intended us to suffer like this. Perhaps we just got caught in the crossfire of an insensitive world, she said. Perhaps the mission is to be kind, extend a hand, make the world better, and discover a cure (insert malady of choice). She feeds me bad jokes, Chicken Soup for my tortured soul and I eat them up in small hurried spoonfuls like a long-starved hunger-striker with a sudden change of heart.

"What do you call children born in a whore-house?"

"I don't know."

"Brothelsprouts."

I chuckled, rather more like a cough to clear a bit of dust in a parched throat. There are more.

"How many synagogue members does it take to change a light bulb?" Again I don't know.

"Change? You want we should change the light bulb? My grandmother donated that light bulb."

During this time Chad got chicken pox. The worst virus you can contract if you are a leukemia patient: no immune system to speak of; no way to fight off infection. Only now that Chad was off of treatment it was okay. Anyway, Idie called and informed me that her daughter, Tamar, had already had them so he could hang with her for a bit as she knew I was so busy being a Don's caretaker. Chad went over Tamar's house to play and next thing I know Idie calls me. She said you aren't going to believe this but I was busy on the phone. When I hung up I went in the other room and there I catch Tamar playing connect the dots on Chad's face with a permanent marker. Yikes. She said he had black marker all over his face connecting one pox to another.

I cracked a smile. A small one, albeit a smile. Perhaps I could make it through one more day.

Chapter 28

To Stress or Not To Stress

Now I know why they call them stress tests. Because they push you to the breaking point. Chad this time, only a few days into 1999. The shape of things to come. Because God thought that I didn't have enough life-altering, joy-sucking, cliff-hanging scenarios to deal with at once, he's now sending them to me in tandem. I'd prefer linear, or none at all if possible, but I've already placed my order and either He's short-staffed or running a slew of backfill orders, I don't know. I just know that UPS hasn't made a delivery in quite some time. But I digress.

They hooked Chad up to about fifteen wires, stuck a huge tube in his mouth, took a clothes pin and closed his nose and told him to start peddling. If I were watching Lucille Ball it might have been hysterical, but it was my son and not funny at all. For forty-five minutes Chad peddled and drooled as the attendant *and* the machine yipped at him to "pump,

pump, come on, faster, you can do it, are we having fun yet?" Why get a personal trainer when you can have a stress test. I'm not sure whose heart was pounding faster, Chad's or mine. I exhausted myself watching him and had to leave the room. By the end he was ready to collapse. He definitely wasn't happy.

The next day, I learned something very important – the true meaning of Stress Test. I can handle leukemia twice and I can handle a husband with brain cancer, but nothing in life could prepare me for this experience.

"What are you doing today, Pen?" Don asked.

"Food shopping," I said.

"Oh good. I'll go with you."

I almost died. Don must be sick if he wants to go food shopping. Everything, I mean EVERYTHING caught his eye to the point that we were inching down the aisles. Finally I snuck away and did the entire store in the span of time within which it took him to get out of aisle one, which is where I found him, reading the ingredients.

He looked up and said, "What's next, Babe?"

"All done. Let's go home."

He never missed me, never knew I left him and $135 later we were out of there. This episode will be published in the next edition of *Redbook* magazines, "Can This Marriage Be Saved?"

As evidence that God doesn't play fair, I got the first blow of the New Year. My family's guardian angel, the one person we could count on to always is there, who never lied, who we could reach out to at any time, about any thing, announced that he was leaving. Dr. Wasserman was leaving for a pharmaceutical company. The desire to do research had forced him out, he said, but I wonder if it wasn't the stress of years of watching so many kids die.

Dr. Wasserman had become a dear family friend, so kind to Chad and then Don, offering the things he could: to make Don more comfortable; to speak with Chad about his Dad being sick; to just be there. I didn't want to go through this wretched, cancer-ridden life without either of them, Don or Dr. Wasserman, and suddenly they were both leaving and I was in this alone. Maybe Chad would never need blood work again, or another stress test. Maybe they'd find a cure for Don's cancer. Or maybe not. Whatever happened, there would be no Don to lean on and no Dr. Wasserman to lead the way. Don even said, "Everyone you could ever count on to be honest and strong for you is on their way out the door. You're on your own, Pen."

I couldn't have felt more isolated if I were on Mars.

During that trying, miserable time, people were always telling me that God only gives you as much as you can handle. But I wonder – if God made me weaker, maybe he wouldn't have given me so much grief and pain. Maybe that was it. Maybe I needed to pray for weakness, not strength, and then watch all this pain fall away.

But it wasn't falling away for Don and hadn't yet for Chad. And so I take their pain, process it, make it my own, or at least something shared between us, like an ice cream float or a chocolate bar, although way less sweet.

Don says, "Pen, I don't want to die. I want to grow old with you and watch our kids grow. I wish there was a cure. I'm not ready to leave you."

He cried. I said nothing, just focused on holding him so he didn't slip away, not yet, just focused on breathing, on making it from one breath to the next, on crying, and our tears, mingling in this shared act of grief. It was all I could do.

Chapter 29

Pot Luck Life

It's hard enough looking to the future, especially as one as bleak and dim as Don's – and mine without him. But when you cloud it with conjectures of the past it becomes a Rubric's Cube of events you have to puzzle through every morning, piece by piece, trying to make them fit, even before you've had your first cup of coffee. They say to live in the present because you expend way too much energy otherwise dwelling on the past and "what iffing" the future. I was giving part of my energy to how Chad's cancer might be lurking around the corner, looking to haul him back down a particularly nasty lane of memories; another to Faith's lost years; another to Don's condition, this new horror threatening to cut my heart out and the very fabric of my family's soul; and of course, more than a few morsels to the part of me that was angry and just plain festering in it. By the time I got my dubious, energy-depleted body up in the morning, I barely had enough to draw sword.

Yet most all of us do this on a daily basis, giving away gobs of energy by failing to call our souls back from their many (redundant) missions, leaving ourselves with only a cupful or two of present-time energy, certainly not enough to face the day.

Which is why when people ask me about Toms River, about the amount of chemical pollutants there, in the air, land and ground water, when they ask me, "don't you think that is the cause of all your problems?" I respond with a shrug. I refuse to dwell on it. If it were true, why don't Faith and I have cancer, or our friends and many neighbors, who drank the same ground water, lived under the same wires, ate the same pesticide-laden tomatoes and breathed the same dense, mercury-laden air. Of course I know of the *canary in the coal mine* effect and it could be that both Chad and Don were just the poor unfortunate canaries. And I'm not pooh-poohing the theories, I'm sure they have merit. But frankly, there was nothing I could really do about it at that juncture. Was it going to change my husband's diagnosis? No. Chad's diagnosis? No. And since I only had a finite amount of energy, I chose to spend it fighting the cancer rather than the cause – and finding ways to end the suffering for my two brave men. Perhaps when I wasn't in the midst of it, maybe years down the road, I might concentrate on that other fight. But right then, I couldn't spare an ounce of intellect or emotion for it. Not while Don's alive days were limited, countable, and mutable. Not while I was making memories.

So I focused my energies on the things I could do. And though I was fearful of what lay ahead for Don, I was petrified of what Chad would face. Don's goal in life was for Chad to be "cured." That meant four more years of being cancer-free before the docs could make that prognosis. The odds were against both of them so I put my limited resources into their comfort, security and safety. It's a big potluck fest, this little life. You never know what's going to be offered you and since can't change yesterday, or control tomorrow, you may as well accept today, sucky as it sometimes was.

Chapter 30

They Fixed Chad, They'll Fix Dad

The cruel cold fact of the matter was, Faith was twelve and Chad was ten and their father was dying. It's just that they didn't know it yet. They had no idea of Don's prognosis and I was petrified of telling them. They simply thought that the doctors fixed Chad, they could do the same for Dad and sat back to enjoy every day of Don's being home with them. Don's only short term goal in those days was to have enough energy to meet them at the school bus at 2:30 so he could make memories with them. His long term goal was to hear Chad's docs declare him the miracle by pronouncing him *cured* which, from all estimates, was four years out. Don would never make it without a miracle of his own.

We'd been through one round and then another of chemo when we hit the dirt. Late February 1999 was proving to be the hardest time yet. First Chad and then Faith got sick, nothing major, just kid stuff, and then me and Don on top of it. The three of us were on the mend, but Don was still down. We thought he just had what Faith and Chad had, but after a while, realized it must be more. My barometer with him was whether he was playing tennis which he hadn't in over two weeks. On February 22nd, we were supposed to take Don to NYU for his fourth and final chemo treatment, but his blood work showed he wasn't strong enough to receive any more.

The days blended together as we waited for him to recover. Don would sleep late then shuffle off to the kitchen for a bad tasting breakfast. Food didn't have the same taste anymore because of the drugs. Eventually, he found his way to the recliner where he slept for the rest of the day. No tennis, no walks, no errands, no nothing, not even meeting the kids at the bus in the afternoon. The doctor told me if I thought he was tired now, wait until he starts radiation.

"The average patient sleeps eighteen to twenty-two hours a day." Dr. June, Don's neurosurgeon said.

"Don's not average," was my reply. However, after that week, I saw him for who he really was. Just a man on chemo. A normal man. A wiped out man. Hmm, an average man.

No matter how weak and tired Don was he found the strength each evening to read to Faith and Chad before bed. They would play this game, Don read one page, Faith read the next, Chad the next, and over and over. After reading he would recite the "Shema." The Shema is an expression of faith, the most important of all the Jewish prayers. It is a quote from the Book of Deuteronomy, the Fifth Book of the Hebrew bible or better known as the Torah. It is traditionally the first thing spoken in the morning and the last thing at night. The children loved when the three of them would sing this very loud and proud each night before bed. My children always remember that special time with their dad, reciting the Shema before they fell asleep each night.

When we got married Don and I decided to keep a kosher home the way he was raised. I was not familiar with this, but enjoyed the tradition. On Friday evenings I would prepare and we would share a Shabbos meal. We all would say the prayers, the *motzee* over the *challah* and Don would say the *kiddish* over the wine/grape juice. Then Don would bless each of us individually, even Muffin. Another beautiful family memory that lingers in Faith and Chad's hearts and minds forever. Years later Faith remarked how so many of her childhood memories had to do with her father blessing us all. What a gift, that memory. I pray that it will last a lifetime and renew their faith in their father's love whenever they most need it.

During that week of waiting, Don was conscious enough to discuss the weighty issues of his limited future. A few weeks prior he had said no respirators, and no "alive at all costs" scenarios. Now he was saying he had to give it a shot.

"I could recover from pneumonia," he said in his own defense.

Now that death was not only knocking, but parting the curtains with its creepy, arthritic fingers and yellowed nails, peering at him through the open window, Don was suiting up, gathering his weaponry and raising all his defenses in preparation for that final battle. Statistically, Don was among a select group who knew with some accuracy when Death would be coming for them. Most of us don't have that luxury. Or is it a bane, that knowing? We know Death's coming for us, somehow, somewhere, perhaps in our sleep, God willing, but not with the same assuredness. Like a prisoner on death row with the date and time announced, Don knew he was going to die, but he was still on his knees, praying for that eleventh hour stay of execution from the governor.

And I right along with him. If I could change the world with the power of my desire, then I know for a fact my husband would be alive today. As it was, there was not much else I could do other than make his life as comfortable as possible and keep the faith because I knew he couldn't do that alone.

So I became the tour director on Don's bus. Actually it gave me something to do so I didn't go insane with worry and blame.

So on February 26, 1999, our family and twenty-one of our dearest friends came to celebrate Faith's thirteenth birthday. Knishes, sweet potatoes, roasted veggies, all homemade by *moi*, lent themselves to our heartfelt feasting. And I used my good china! We shared some poignant memories together even though Don was out of it, so sedated, and even quieter than normal. How many ways could a heart break? The question, like a Zen koan, haunted my days. To most, it was an imponderable, unanswerable truth, but not to me. I knew the answer. There were a million ways to Sunday to break a heart and then some. There just weren't as many ways to put it back together.

Earlier in the day, I had asked Don if he still wanted to do Faith's celebration or maybe postpone it until later.

"Until when, Pen?" he replied. "This could be a good day for me. I might not be at Faith's next birthday. I really want today to happen for my sake and for Faith's." To which he added, "I just didn't want you to have to work so hard after the week you've had."

Finally, someone noticed. For one brief moment, my role as the entertainment director, event coordinator, nurse, chauffeur, and memory-maker-Mom was acknowledged. I hadn't looked upon the preparation of that dinner as a chore. What was tiresome was the need to be "it" for everyone with generally no recognition and no time, I mean, NO TIME, to myself.

A dear friend asked me, "How are you doing, Pen?" And I said, "Who cares? It isn't really important how I'm doing. Maybe it'll be again some day, but not now." Although, that's not really what I meant to say. I *was* important: there was just no time for me to remind myself.

And Don knew it. The magic of our relationship was that I could vent my frustration to him and he would understand. I told him I was disappointed in him for getting sick. Not angry, just disappointed.

"How would you feel after twenty-four years of being you're everything if I just checked out? You know – people leave each other all the time. It's bad. But at least they can still talk. Not with you, though. And I have a lot to say."

I'd do very badly with the situation, Pen. Even worse than you. You have friends, family a sense of humor, resources to survive. I only have you. I only ever wanted you. And I only want you now. I don't want anyone else to take me for radiation, or give me my meds. Maybe it's selfish, but it's you, Pen. The only one who knows the real me."

Then he said as he did so many times since he's gotten sick, "I'm sorry, Pen. Sorry for prolonging this pain with my illness."

Enough to melt your heart, right? Had mine not been shattered and crazy glued back together so many damn times that moment would have done it for me. Instead, I shook him off and announced my own desires.

"I want to have an affair. You disappointed me so I'll disappoint you."

Don did his best to hide a smile and indulged me. "Well, who do you want to have an affair with?"

"Sure – now you make me date. Now that I'm past my prime and everyone is either bald, overweight or losing their teeth."

Don laughed, and then sighed. "I don't envy you, Pen. It'll be hard to learn again. I'll be at peace. It'll be you who's suffering."

Again I say, "Who cares."

Chapter 31

Apparently, Someone Does Care. . .

And his name was Chad Juros. Unbeknownst to me, Chad entered me in a Mom of the Year Contest. In one hundred words or less, he needed to describe why I should win. Here it is:

Mom of the Year Contest
April 3, 1999
Chad Juros, age 11

I have leukemia and my mom kept me alive. From the beginning she never left my side, cared for me, took me to appointments, kissed, fed and held me and never dropped me at the hospital and left me there alone like other kid's parents did. I got leukemia in 1991 and again in 1995 and she lived with me at the hospital for over a year. The best was waking up and knowing she was right next to me. She made me laugh. She would not let me see how sad she was and kept trying to keep me smiling.

(98 words)

(And now my dad has brain cancer and she is doing this for him.)

Because of Chad's write up, I won – dinner for two and flowers – and a thank you from my son no money could buy.

Through these years Chad's magic career was soaring. Everyone wanted a piece of the healthy magic boy who survived cancer twice, whose Dad had taught him the magic and who himself was now dying. It seemed that all wanted to be part of the story, to feel they helped in some way. Added to that, however, Chad happened to be great at magic. He had the skill, talent, ability, charisma and looks. He put on a fabulous entertaining show so he was in huge demand for block parties, birthday celebrations, family reunions and all types of performances. The phone would ring nonstop for this 10 year old magic boy to entertain. In addition to being a caretaker I had taken on the pleasure of being Chad's agent/manager. That, along with all my other duties, was a labor of love.

Chapter 32

Ay Ay Captain

The kids just didn't get it. And I hadn't been man enough to tell them. They both asked Don on separate occasions when he was going back to work. They knew we sold the dental office but didn't realize what that meant.

Chad: "You mean you aren't going to be a dentist anymore?"

Faith: "You mean you're not going back to the office?"

Don answered, "Who knows," but said he doubted it.

For the first time Chad realized something was up. I knew because he told me, "Daddy sleeps all the time." I couldn't, wouldn't, wasn't ready to admit that the gig was up either to them or myself. So I did what any overly
concerned, overly-optimistic, controlling mother would under the circumstances. I planned a little trip.

It was mid-March and still cold in New Jersey so guess what? St. Thomas, here we come. We went over the kids' spring break from school and it was a fabulous trip, swimming, snorkeling, lounging on the beach, being totally pampered. Don looked and felt great, although slept most of the day, and we had a brief respite from tragedy.

As we boarded our little nine-seat commuter flight home, the captain looked us over and said:

"Chad, you go sit in front with me. I need a co-pilot." (That was sooo cool.) "Don, you go sit in the middle. Penny and Faith, you go sit in the very back."

I reply, in my whiny voice, "Mr. Captain, are you doing that because of my weight?"

"No," he said, chuckling, "because of your height. There's no leg room in the back and you're short.

"Yeah, right. Uh-huh."

"Why, you're not even fat."

"Oh how sweet. Want to be my new best friend?"

The captain laughs, looks at Don and asks, "Is she always like this? She's funny."

"Always," Don replies. "Pen, get on the plane."

Our flight home was as perfect as the entire vacation. We didn't want it to end. Of course, once we touched down, the nightmare began anew. There were messages from my mom that she was flying to Arizona to be with my grandfather who was very sick – his kidneys were failing and his blood pressure too low. I was very close to my grandparents. There really was no good way to come home.

The next morning, Don and I left for simulation, a procedure they do before brain radiation. The docs up at HUP informed us that they were starting Don on radiation the next day and that he'd need to continue until April 30th. They took Don away and left me reading in the waiting room. A bit later, I looked up to see Don being wheeled down the hall with a mask over his face and wrapped in a sheet. *What was this?* I couldn't believe Don could look so bad so fast. A second ago we were snorkeling and playing tennis. I flew out of my chair and ran after Don's wheelchair. I touched the back of his shoulder and he turned. *Thank God!* It wasn't him. It just looked like him from the side and back. I fell apart.

The nurse came over and said, "Oh you poor thing. How upsetting. That man does look like your husband." She pointed down the hall. "You're husband is actually back in that room over there. I noticed he walked with a bounce to his step. He's just fine."

I gaped at her, open-mouthed, and watched her wheel the unknown Don look-alike down the hall . . . to Don's future.

I wanted to go back to BC – before cancer – but that world was so small, barely a speck in my memory, I didn't even know what the heck it was all about. I was scared, frustrated, lonely, worried and tired – tired of being head cheerleader, tired of making social plans I had to cancel because Don was exhausted or didn't remember committing to them, tired of watching our lives self-destruct. I probably could have used a shrink at that time, but I refused to seek medical treatment. Instead, I self-medicated, living on Yodels, Tastycakes and Tootsie Rolls (I never met a chocolate I didn't like) and sometimes even that wasn't enough. After years of not sleeping because I was afraid I'd wake up to Chad dead, I was preparing myself for not sleeping so I wouldn't wake up to Don being dead. My life was falling apart for a second time and, but for the dying, Don's was better than ever. He told me that, "this is the happiest he has ever been in his life." After all those years he was finally getting along beautifully with everyone, socializing, spending quality time with his family, traveling, like his retirement years, doing everything he always wanted to do if he had the chance. Too bad he had to get the death sentence to do it.

Chapter 33

Puffs Plus

It was already May 1999. We had never lied to our children, and I honestly didn't want to start now, but how does any mother tell a child their daddy is dying? In the beginning, the experts had told us to wait, why worry those months or hopefully years before we needed. But Don's full resection only bought him a bit of time. And the worst was closing in fast. It was time to start worrying them. This week's MRI showed "abnormalities." The doctors were "concerned."

"Does that mean it' back?" Faith asked.

"We don't know, but if it is, it doesn't mean its over," I said.

"But you both have to leave again to get him treatment, don't you?"

"If it's back, we do."

"Will you both come home from the hospital?"

"That's our plan."

"Talk about bad luck. Two cancers, one family. What's that about?" Faith asked.

I had no answers for her, but at least she was open enough to ask. Chad, on the other hand, didn't want to know nothin' from nothin', especially when it came to losing his best friend. And like an unwanted stranger found lurking in the bedroom closet, Chad felt just thinking of cancer was dangerous because it could signal the return of his own. And so he shrugged it off, turned away and refused to even acknowledge it. I cut him a break because he was only ten, and four years from walking away from his own disastrous past, but it was difficult. He was a survivor, my boy, but he wanted his dad to be there when he did it. Who could blame him? His dad was his number one magic fan, his mentor, his best buddy in the world.

One night, I went to bed at 9:30 while Don was watching *Star Trek* in bed next to me. I woke up when I heard him shut the TV, but I didn't move or make a noise. Next thing I know I feel him in the dark, covering me and tucking me in real tight. Then he kissed my forehead and whispered, "I'm sorry I have to die and leave you. Who's going to tuck you in now? You don't deserve this, Pennybabe."

I never opened my eyes or said a word; the tears just flowed.

The next week we were sitting outside on the porch swinging in the love seat and I asked Don "What do you think is going to happen with my life?"

Don paused and after some thought said, "I don't know, Pen, but whatever happens, no matter where you are, even if you remarry, please each and every night tell me what happened with you and the kids that day. I'll be listening. And when we meet again in heaven, I'll be all caught up."

Then he said, "I'm serious, Pen. Keep my email address and send me an email. When I'm in heaven and hear, 'you've got mail,' I'll know it's from you.'"

To this day, I still send him an email almost every night.

Chapter 34

Brain Stuff

Seventy weeks. Seventy lousy weeks. That's what you get with this disease once it's been diagnosed. Don's lost a lot of hair because of the radiation and was worried about "looking like a cancer patient" so he went and got a buzz cut. I continually tell him how good he looked, hair or no hair. *Rah, rah, sis-boom-bah.* (Just don't ask me to do a cartwheel or a split.) He smiled, so I guess it was helping. He slept a whole lot and still played tennis although he said he wasn't winning anymore. It didn't matter, as long as he was playing.

Faith asked me, "Are you born with a brain tumor or does it just grow as you get older?"

I didn't know how to answer that. It was possible, wasn't it; to be born with the shadow of a seed of a malignant cell that one day blossomed into a full grown tumor. Or maybe you just breathed in the wrong air, ate too much pesticide-tainted food, or swam in polluted water. Who the hell knows? I just wish I had something to tell my daughter to alleviate her million and one fears.

"Am I too old to get leukemia?" she asked. "I'm considered safe now, right?"

I wanted to say, "Define safe," so I could couch it in equivocal terms that would buy me some slack if I were wrong, but still give her the comfort she so desperately sought, but I didn't dare. She was too sharp. She'd nail me to the wall with her questions until I cracked and told her what I thought she was still too young to hear: that there were no guarantees, that life itself was inherently unsafe, and that struggle mightily as we did as parents, we couldn't always keep our children safe. So I said nothing, just nodded and hoped the stupid, sympathetic smile on my face was enough to assuage her myriad and constant fears.

Elaine Geller, Rabbi Geller's wife posed this trivia question to me: "How many times a day does Penny show the Juros' insurance card?"

Actually, I was thinking of having it laminated and wearing it like an employee I.D. card around my neck. It does pretty much sum up my whole *raison d'etre* in this lifetime.

Oy.

Chapter 35

Let the Days Be What They Are

I would forward a prayer to God on Don's behalf except He still wasn't listening to me. I don't know what He was listening to, maybe classic rock, maybe oldies, but whatever; it had nothing to do with our stuff. I was brought up to believe that if I did everything right I'd be rewarded. Well, I'd lived up to my end of the bargain so what had happened? I didn't want my husband to die and leave me. I was neither brave enough nor strong enough for the aftershocks. But in spite of my fears, at that point all I could pray for was Don's peaceful, dignified death. Unfortunately, God wasn't even sport enough for that simple request. What a cheapskate.

My newest friends and confidants became the brain tumor support group on the Internet. It's a group of brain cancer patients and their caretakers who communicate via email. The hospital plugged me into this group and other than the care they'd offered my husband, it was the best thing they could have done for me. This group of people numbering somewhere close to a thousand was as fungible as a blade of grass. People came and went as their loved ones came and went. There was absolutely no reason to be on the list once your spouse or parent or child had died; it was just too depressing. But while they were alive – and dying – there was nothing like the list to help you maintain your sanity. The list was replete with wise men and women, hundreds of modern day sages, worn down, the way water wears down rock, by the circumstances of their lives. You watch them erode until everything unnecessary has fallen away and only the essentials remain: the beauty, the light, the compassion.

One of a thousand wise men on that list told me his story of his once vital father dying of glioblastoma multiforme iv – gbm – Don's cancer. He required round-the-clock nursing care. The father was in constant pain. The son, on a whim, gave the nurses the day off and a much needed break. He spent the day tending to his father's myriad and constant needs. However, instead of viewing it as a chore, he looked upon it as a gift, a chance to live every single moment to its fullest potential, to see the beauty even in the pain. "Even his trips to the bathroom every forty-five minutes took on a poignancy that I had not experienced before. I urge you all to live every minute . . . and let the days be what they are."

A divine soul of my friend, Deidre, had forwarded some of my "why me" emails to a friend of hers going through a similarly rough patch. The friend, having talked to her pastor on numerous occasions regarding her own difficult circumstances, relayed her pastor's words back to me.

We all have our time or moment, our divine purpose, the reason for which we were created. Maybe it's to be a CEO or a surgeon, to hit a home run or support our country in battle. Or maybe it's to hold the hand of someone who's scared, or to take care of a loved one who's dying. Whatever it is, that's why we're here – to rise to the challenge. We may never know why or when or if there are more challenges to come, but that's life. Perhaps Penny was put here to take care of Don and Chad. I don't know her, but I'd say both of those lives have been blessed with a special wife and mother in Penny. So accept what you can't control, and face all the heartaches with love, courage, dignity and no regrets.

Mind you, I never met this woman, but it was refreshing to hear a different perspective. It changes absolutely nothing and almost everything.

Chapter 36

Seize the Day

June 4, 1999. Admittedly, it caught me off guard, the first one. So much so that I didn't know what was happening. I asked Don if he wanted to go out that night, but he said he was really tired and wanted to pass. So he and Chad watched, *The Truman Show* and I took Faith to a bat mitzvah, and then tried to rustle up a friend to go to the movies with. No one was available, and lucky, too, because at 7 o'clock, Don came in and said, "Pen, something's wrong with my jaw. Call Rob Fiedler."

I looked up and jumped about a thousand feet. "Oh my God, Don, you had a stroke. Your face is hanging way down."

"Pen, call Rob and tell him to get here fast. I was chewing gum and I knocked my jaw out of line is all."

I called Rob. I think they were the only people left in America who didn't have call waiting. "Don, it's busy."

"Call Laura and tell her to go get him."

Laura lived next door and could easily run over. I called, but no answer. I called Ivy who also lived nearby and the babysitter answered. I called Jaime and Terry answered.

"Please run down the street and tell Rob it's an emergency."

Meanwhile, I called NYU. I got their answering machine. Five minutes later, Rob called and I said, "Don wants you to come here and put his jaw back in alignment."

"I'm leaving now," was all he said.

He was pulling up the driveway when NYU called back. "Is this a reaction to the carboplatin," I asked.

"No, Penny," Dr. Grub said. "This is a seizure."

"Oh my God."

"What side is it?"

"Right."

"Are his hands or legs shaking?"

"No."

"Can he talk?"

"His speech is slurred."

"Let me talk to him."

Don took the phone, but could hardly speak. Dr. Grub told him to take an extra anti-seizure medication and get some Valium."

Just as I hung up, Rob walked in the door.

"This isn't his jaw, Pen. This is a seizure.

"The doctor said to get Valium."

"I have some at home. Call Marcia and tell her to bring it, or I'll go get it."

"I'll meet her at WaWa," I said.

"Go. I'll stay with Don. He can't be alone."

As soon as I got back, I saw the worst of it through the window: Rob holding Don in a bear hug and Don flipping out. I rushed into the house.

"Pen, it got real bad while I was on the phone with Grub. He says give him five milligrams of Valium and if there's no relief in an hour, take him to the ER."

Don took ten milligrams. During all this, Chad rushed into the room, took one look at his Dad and rushed into our room where he hid in the corner.
It was 8:30 p.m. and Don needed to get through the next hour. Rob said it wasn't a grand mal seizure, just in the brain, so if Don could stand the pain it would be over in an hour. Don kept waiting for me to go in the other room and then he'd scream from the pain.

"This is out of my league, Pen. I've never seen anything like this," Rob said.

"But why is it happening? The MRI was clear."

"It's the cells around the tumor reacting to the chemo," he told me. "It could happen with radiation, too.

It could happen for thirty years and you'd never see a growth, or it could be the beginning of a growth. But I'm pretty sure it's a reaction."

I was shaking all over and since Rob couldn't do any more for Don, he focused on calming me down. At 9:15 p.m., Don had the worst of it, a horrible, intense spasm, like a tremor following an earthquake. I shuddered right along with him.

By 9:30 p.m. it was over. Don looked normal, just really sleepy. We called NYU and Grub said to give him one more seizure medication and put him to bed. I checked on Chad who'd fallen asleep in the corner of our bedroom and carried him off to bed. Rob left. I put Don to bed and collapsed. I had told Grub and Rob that I'd never reacted like this with Chad; this was much scarier.

"Get ready," Grub said. "This is only the beginning."

Thank God for Rob Fiedler. He held all of us up that night. Years later I started referring to him as my savior. No matter how bad things got, Rob was always there to cushion the fall.

Chapter 37

The Rollercoaster

May 2, 1999. After eight years of doctors and hospitals you'd think I would have learned that what they say isn't always the case and what they think isn't always the right thought. And so it was the latest MRI results that proved the tumor was under control and not growing. I was waiting for Don to finish radiation and talking to a friend who had just relayed some good news so I was smiling.

Just then, Don came up and said the doctors wanted to talk to us. Suddenly I couldn't swallow.

They put us in an examining room and had the audacity to leave us there for an hour. We didn't talk or look at each other once. Don sat there and I paced while memories of Chad's dual incarcerations and the incessant waiting on test results threatened to take my knees out at every turn.

Finally, Dr. Meite came in and without looking either one of us in the eye said,

"I'm sorry. The Fellow who read your MRI was wrong. The Attending looked at the films and saw abnormalities, more "brightness" than in January, but no tumors yet. If so, we'd go in and cut them out. But they aren't sure what it is so they don't know what to do with it. It could even be inflammation."

"Now you know why I didn't get too excited last week when you told me the good news," Don said. I had to admire him, he was so calm.

"Can they do gamma knife radiation?" he asked.

"No, not yet," Dr. Meite said. "You'll talk to Dr. June tomorrow. He'll lay out your options. At this point, we don't think you should do anything other than radiation."

"I'm not going to just sit back and let it grow until you're sure."

"I'm sorry."

Don looked at me in exasperation. I was shaking again and my tongue felt thick, but the words came out strong, precise and authoritative.

"I never want a fellow to read Don's scans again. You were wrong. I would have stopped you right then if I knew. Chad wasn't treated by a Fellow oncologist and neither will Don be. Whether it saves Don's life or only buys him ten more minutes, I only want the best. You won't play with me or our emotions like that again."

"Penny, I'm sorry for the emotional roller coaster. It was not my intent. We want to do another MRI around Mother's Day. I'm sorry for that as well."

"Look, Dr. Meite. I've spent three different years as an in-patient at CHOP with Chad on Mother's Day, four New Year's Eves, and four birthdays. I've found that the pain comes when it comes and doesn't concern itself with holidays."

He just looked at me, sheepish and sad. I walked out of the room.

When we left, the very nice receptionist stamped our parking ticket and wrote "Chad Juros" in the ledger.

"It's Don, not Chad. Same family, different cancer."

"I'm sorry for the mix-up," the receptionist said. "I just remember what a great kid Chad was."

"Seems like there are a lot of mix-ups in this department," I said.

"I know sorry doesn't help. You've had way too much to handle."

To prove how upset I was, walking out, I stepped on the scale. I'd dropped eleven pounds in a week.

And me, Miss Weight Conscious, always trying to drop a pound or two, reacted not as if I'd just won the lottery, but as if even that very thought depressed me.

Don said, "Geez, Penny, until a minute ago, your weight was one of the most important things in the world."

"It doesn't matter, Don, if I'm fat or thin. It won't make you live any longer and it won't take away my pain now."

Don put his arm around me. "I've been trying to tell you that all along, Pen."

Driving home we didn't talk until we hit the A.C. Expressway.

"You know, Pen. I'm not going down without a fight."

"I didn't think so. It's not your style."

"And I'm not going to take their word for it and just not do anything. I'm calling Dr. Grub and Dr. June for their opinions, and maybe some of my original doctors, too. I'll go out kicking and screaming. On the other hand, it's you I worry about. You don't deserve this."

"I'm tough. Somehow I'll get through it," I said, not taking my eyes off the road. "But you won't."

"I'll be dead, Pen. It's you and the kids who'll have to live with the pain."

Stop this ride. I want to get off.

Chapter 38

Location, Location, Location

June 8, 1999. My parents came over to watch the kids so we could attend a Brain Tumor Symposium at the Hospital of the University of Pennsylvania (HUP). About two hundred people were there and counting Don, only three had bald heads. I was heartened at first until they said that almost all of the entire audience was caretakers. Dr. June, Don's neurosurgeon and the Chief at HUP, spoke, as did Linda Stevens, a social worker, and several others.

Basically, we learned what we'd been afraid of: that brain cancer was on the rise and it had the deadliest and quickest kill rate with one to two years estimated survival, but closer to one. They discussed clinical trials, how it was extending three months of life in some cases and that so far radiation was the only known treatment that worked after surgery to remove what you could. Some chemos were working, but the data was still shy; very few drugs could cross the blood barrier into the brain.

They discussed a method for "grading" tumors. Don had a four, the worst, which means we shouldn't go looking for miracles because there were none. His tremors would get worse as would his balance as he continued to weaken overall. (Lately, we hadn't just been holding hands; I'd been holding him up.) His mouth would get drier, his fatigue immeasurable, and worst of all, his short term memory would suffer drastically. The more symptoms, the quicker he'd fail. Unfortunately, he had tons: several years' worth of frozen shoulders, numbness, tingling in the fingers, extreme personality changes, lethargy, and bizarre behavior. He probably had the lower grade tumor for many years and was now in the final stages. And with tumors, like real estate, it was all about location. In Don's case they got the entire tumor out, but they were one hundred percent sure that there were cells still in his brain running amok. The full resection gained him quality of life, no more. Estimated time after surgery was eighty weeks. Don was thirty-two weeks into it. Some of Don's doctors talked to us afterwards about other treatment possibilities, none of them cures, maybe just buying a few precious, swollen moments. They talked about doing what was best for our family and recommended Don picking a treatment and not looking back, just focusing on spending time with loved ones while he still had it, that the summer would be a gift and to take it. We didn't hear a single word of encouragement the whole evening. It was the worst.

A week passed and Faith was inducted into the National Honor Society. My father and I cried through the entire thing while Don, Chad and my mom smiled. *Living each moment.*

Also that week, Chad told me he believed God helped him through his leukemia twice, and that he helped Don get rid of his tumor and Faith with her asthma. I asked him if God helped me do anything.

"Yes. He helped you be my mommy and get me through all that stuff and made you the type that makes me smile even when I didn't want to. He picked you to be healthy so you can help us all."

Dear God, give me the strength to be the woman my son thinks I am.

June 10, 1999, and Don had three new tumors, maybe five. It was no longer just one tumor in the frontal lobe; they'd crossed over the corpus callosum, the midline of the brain, and scattered in all directions like an army of ants, sending out their reconnaissance scouts two, four, six at a time while behind them stood hundreds more. The resected tumor was still gone, nothing there but a big yawning whole in Don's grey matter. But before making its undignified exit, it tossed its cells in its silent insidious way, like seeds in the wind, leaving us to deal with its fecund, deadly fallout. Dr. June called it White Dot Disease because the white dots on the MRI looked like cancerous tumors. They couldn't go in and operate because they were either too small or in an unfortunate location. I called it pigeon poop.

Perhaps chemo could still shrink them, but MAB wouldn't work and neither would a gamma boost because Don had cancer in five areas and they only work in up to three.

"This isn't my end talk, by no means," Dr. June said. "I hate that talk. You still have many days ahead. But do it now. This summer. While the kids are home from school."

Don turned white, closed his eyes and took a series of deep breaths, then turned to me.

"Why aren't you floored," he asked me.

"Because I knew something was up. I never expected to hear five, never expected to hear crossed over the corpus callosum, never expected to hear inoperable, but I knew from how you've been acting something was up."

"Why are you always right, Pen?"

"Boy do I wish I could be wrong this time."

Dr. June scheduled an MRI appointment for three months later. While driving home, Don made a list of names he wanted to send MRI's to and a list of questions. We stopped at the mall to eat and walking the food court it finally hit me – so hard I had to sit down. Don ordered three pieces of pizza, two for him and one for me, and he ate all three while I just sat there, dazed.

Chapter 39

The Shape of Things to Come

I've always been an advocate for the present, for living life in the moment, leave 'em laughing when you can. And while the first thirty-four years of my life I had the world by the tail on a downward roll, the next eight hadn't quite gone according to plan. And so it was with a sense of dread that I accompanied Don to Dr. June's office to hear his advice on Don's recommended course of treatment from here on in, whenever "in" might be.

Before we met with Dr. June, Don had an appointment with the social worker, Linda Stevens. Don liked a lot of what she had said at the symposium we attended a few nights before and wanted her advice on a treatment. I was surprised when Don asked me to go with him.

"I want you to hear her opinion, too, Pen. But your opinion matters more."

Even more surprising was that Linda remembered us even though we hadn't seen her since Don was diagnosed. As Don was rehashing his plans, Linda put up her hand to stop him and said,

"Penny, you're a very generous, supportive woman."

"I haven't said a word yet."

"No, but all I'm hearing from Don is how much you've done for him and the kids."

I started sniffling and choked out a "thank you, but anyone would do the same."

"I see hundreds of families a year. Most of the women are selfish, angry and not willing to do what you're allowing Don to do. You're letting him make all the decisions because it's his life and you support every one of those decisions. You haven't had a break from the caretaker business in eight years. By now, one would think you'd feel a little less selfish."

I cried. Her words returned to me at least my shadow, a huge improvement over my former invisibility. She then gave us some very concrete ways of talking to the kids, how their summer schedule would go and how we should include them in the decision-making. She suggested Don tape record messages, create emails to be sent later, and make journals for them both. She remembered Faith as being brilliant and intuitive and thought she was ready to hear the news. Not Chad though.

She remembered our supportive families. "Tell them over and over that whatever happens in your life you won't face it alone. Tell them that you have a very strong family and that no one will abandon them ever, that not everything in their life is quicksand."

Don told her he felt better about himself than he had in the last ten years. "If I die tomorrow, I know nothing's been left unsaid. I've got a good relationship with everyone. And I made my peace for the first time in a long time with God." When he was done, I asked to see her alone for fifteen minutes.

Before he left, Linda said, "Don, all I've heard here for the last hour was of the amazing love you have for Penny and your children. Lots of times couples come in and fight, but you held hands the entire time. You're a mature, generous, thoughtful, self-involved, wise man and all your priorities are in order. Something you don't see that often. You'll be fine."

Don was crying when he left the room.

"Penny, you're about to break. It's so obvious. When I talk you don't look at me; you look around the room. You can't handle listening to one more thing. But you need some kind of break because the worst is yet to come. You should go away for the weekend."

"I can't leave Don or Faith now," I said to my shoes. "They're both too fragile."

"Then go for a day, but get someone to watch Don."

"No, he's become too dependent on me. He'll say 'only if Penny can go.' When I do go out to lunch or breakfast to meet friends he always asks when I'll be home and tells me to hurry back."

"Then get some drugs. Something mild to help you sleep and stop your shaking."

I hadn't noticed it, but I was shaking. Before I left she explained to me what the coming death would be like. I can't say if her explanation stilled my hand.

Don and I talked about the drugs on the way home and he said only I knew if I needed them. "You always get nervous when you talk to others. Maybe she misinterpreted your shaking.

If drugs would have been enough I would have taken them all. But I knew it wasn't what I needed. Driving home, a bird took a crap on our windshield and Don said, "Hey, Pen, even your car has White Dot Disease. Maybe my MRI dots are just bird poop."

Don't we wish?

Chapter 40

Funky White Stuff

Summer was a week away, but no one in the Juros house felt like celebrating. The news of Don's five new "little" tumors rocked us pretty hard. *Little,* like cute, lovable friends. Even Dr. Wasserman, the epitome of calm was unnerved by this one. He called, asking about the guys. He had reports of a Chad-sighting the week before – Dr. Hammer said Chad looked "great" – but he'd heard nothing about Don. I filled him in, "doing well, just the side-effects from the chemo, plus the five new little ones."

I heard a gasp on the other end.

"Bob, what's up? You're usually pretty calm."

"This is bad. Did he tell you that?"

"Yep. Stable; small; inoperable."

"Did they cross over the corpus callosum?"

"Yep."

"This isn't good, Penny. I'm sure you know that. Once they scatter like that they're hard to treat."

"I know," I said, barely a whisper.

I passed the phone over to Don and Don later reported Dr. Wasserman told him about a new trial in gene therapy. He told Don to call Jefferson the next day. Before he signed off, he gave me his email address at work and told me to keep him posted.

When Don and I got married, he promised me the world. In those last days he'd repeatedly tell me, "It's a small world." There's an old Jewish saying: *from strength to strength.* That was us – Don and I. And soon it was just going to be me. What happens when only one was left, when agony was on the rise and ecstasy on the decline; when choices were limited by the mundane: balance, mobility, the ability to focus for more than ten seconds at a time. What happens when there's nothing left to do, but sit idly by as your life slips to the ground? Time was speeding up; the lamp lighting my way was flickering. And when my life's love's light was extinguished, where would my strength be then?

Don and I flew to Duke in North Carolina the last Wednesday in June for an MRI and a PET scan – superimposed and co-registered – like an X-Box game. That's how Dr. Freid liked them done and we couldn't find a closer hospital to do it. The PET showed two things (Dr. Harry's words): 1) "that there are many new dots, too numerous to count, scattered across both hemispheres" and that they looked, "very funky"; and 2) the white dots weren't necrosis, but an increase "in metabolism and hypermetabolic."

Translation (my words): the white dots were either cancerous tumors, or Don was toxic from all the chemo and radiation, causing his brain to spread out – clinging sloppily to a chaise lounge at poolside after ingesting one too many frozen margaritas – and go kaplooey. I felt my translation, although less scientific in nature, was a more visually accurate depiction of what was happening inside my husband's head.

Dr. Harry told us to fly back home, that he'd show Dr. Allan the new scans with the "chicken pox" effect and ask him to do a biopsy. If he ruled out tumors, Don could get MAB. If he didn't, well....

Dr. Harry spent two hours with us. He was kind, sweet, friendly, professional, and funny – a pleasure.

He told Don, "Don't let anyone write you off yet. Not until we know what these funky things are. You certainly don't look like a man dying of brain cancer. You look real good. Let's hope it's nothing."

Out of seven opinions, Dr. Harry's was the only hopeful one. All the other doctors wrote us off with comments like, "it looks bad. See us in three months to see how much worse it got."

And then there was Dr. Grub who treated Don with such a supreme lack of respect and caring, the likes of which I'd never seen.

"Yes, Mr. Juros," the receptionist said. "Dr. Grub got your message. I don't know why he's not calling you back."

Not only do they write you off, they don't have the decency to return calls. Dying was hard enough. Being disrespected just added insult to injury.

Chapter 41

Hallelujah

June 25, 1999. I couldn't wait until this lousy month was over. It had been one heartache after another. Maybe I should have gotten a part time job, something to get me out of the house and my own head while I was at it. That night, I walked by the bedroom and Don was sitting on the edge of the bed with a simple sort of grin on his face. No one else would have even noticed it, but I did. He looked like a crazo. Like a weird old man in an old age home, sorry and strange. This was the man I couldn't wait to run to at the end of the day. Now I have nothing to say to him. One minute he was alert, sharp, and coherent. The next he was incoherent, practically crawling instead of walking. He said he felt like he was walking in potholes. We were waiting to hear from Duke, but I was hitting the wall. I wanted it to be over. Maybe I could start to heal.

A week later we were flying back to Duke to get their opinion first hand. The flight was delayed, but almost empty which made up for it. But, just our luck, there was a holy roller sitting directly in front of us, screaming at the top of her lungs. "Praise the Lawd." during the entire take off and landing, so loud that the flight attendants had to come over and calm her down. She was hysterical, scared out of her mind, going berserk. We were busting laughing. The pilot said it should be smooth sailing, but it wasn't. He hit a real bad patch of turbulence for maybe fifteen minutes and we were all shaking. Don yells out, "Praise the Lawd," and the stewardess gave him a look like, "Don't you start, too."

A bit later I turned to Don and asked, "Does it look like I could use a haircut?"

Don said, "Well, Dear," - he never calls me Dear – "that's hard to say. Does it look like I could use one?" He took off his hat and exhibited his bald head. I was plotzing (dying), so I just shut up and ate my snacks, excellent by airport standards.

The hotel suite was huge, dishwasher, coffee maker, microwave, two TVS, all the comfies of home. There was a big shopping center right on the premises so we stocked up on munchies for Don because once he started steroids he would go bonkers. There was also a breakfast buffet, free until 10 AM, but I was going to have to move old Donald along here or he'd snooze and lose. Don was to check in at noon at the hospital the next day.

Praise the Lawd, we had made it.

Chapter 42

Flash Dance

Just before nine the next morning, Don had the first of what would be eleven grand mal seizures that day. Now I've seen some terrible things with Chad, but this was a few degrees north on the horrific scale. I was getting dressed and Don was sitting across from me reading the paper and eating a bagel when without warning, he just fell over onto the floor in the prayer position.

Thinking he was fooling around, I said, "What are you doing? Get up." But before the words even left my mouth I knew something wasn't right.

I picked up the phone and called for an ambulance, then ran out in the hall and yelled for help. He'd fallen down and I couldn't turn him over. He was foaming at the mouth and his entire body was twitching and jerking all over the place. I watched as his eyeballs rolled up in his head and his wagging tongue did flip-flops in his mouth.

As luck would have it, I'd been getting dressed when Don hit the floor so I quick threw on a pair of pants and was buttoning them when five paramedics flew in the door. I wonder how many half-naked women these guys see in the line of duty.

Flustered, I told them that Don had brain cancer, that he was having a grand mal seizure, and that this was his first. Mind you, I reported all this without a shirt or a bra, proving conclusively that it's not the clothes that make the man, or woman, in my case. One of the paramedics shut the door and told me to finish getting dressed. When we got Don on the stretcher, he started to revive. One of the paramedics asked him his name, but he didn't know it. Once in the ambulance, he seized again, although this time it was worse – as if that were possible.

I was up front with the driver who was doing eighty-five miles an hour while the EMT in the back was yelling for him to drive faster. Don was thrashing like a fish sans H2O which precluded the EMT from finding a vein. At the hospital, despite the anti-seizure meds, Don began seizing all over again. He had eleven grand mal seizures in all, including one cardiac arrest. During the course of it, they kicked me out of the room and told me to get his parents. By two o'clock it was over. Don's heart rate was good and they took him for a CT scan. Afterwards, he threw up all over me and the nurse. I just caught it the way I did with the kids and mumbled something meant to be soothing, whether to him or me, I don't know. The rest of the day he spent sleeping on and off, but his wakeful times were at best incoherent.

The doctor said the CT scan showed that he either had a stroke on the right side (the original tumor was on the left) or there was a new tumor so big that the swelling caused the seizure. At 9 PM, they moved him to a step down room which comes with less monitoring than ICU, but more than average in-patient monitoring. He had a private room, but I couldn't stay with him. The nurse told me he was scheduled for surgery, but she wasn't sure if it was for an emergency craniotomy to get the tumor out or just the biopsy we'd come for. She couldn't ask Dr. Alan because he was still in surgery (since 5:30 a.m. – talk about a brutal schedule) and hadn't had a chance to look at the CT scan yet. She told me to be back early.

The whole night, Don kept repeating, "Was it bad? What happened? Do the kids know? How bad was it?" over and over. As little things started coming back to him he asked me why I was so calm. (I'm a good actress.) He still didn't know his name, but he new mine and the year (which at that point was more than

I knew). Before I left, he finally knew his name, where he lived, where he was and that he had eleven grand mal seizures. Honestly, that's got to be some kind of record.

The scene at the hospital couldn't have gotten worse if I scripted it. My quiet, dignified husband told me he had to go to the bathroom. The nurse said no, he was too sedated, and handed him a bedpan. Well, he may be quiet, but he's no pushover. He didn't like it so he stood up – with me saying, "no, no, no" – and proceeded to poop all over me, my shoes, my clothes, no control, just let loose, and this after vomiting on me earlier. His entire body was tremoring. I can't believe I didn't gag or get sick, just stood there, trying to catch it or help him somehow.

When Don finally became coherent, I told him about my flash dance for the paramedics at the hotel suite. He laughed and said, "They won't ever forget you."

Later the paramedics stopped in to say hi to Don – or maybe to check to see if I was still dressed – and I said, "Remember me? The flasher?"

The EMT replied, "How could I forget. That was shocking."

"I know you've seen a lot, but maybe not everything until today, huh?"

"Actually," the EMT said, "it was a nice way to start the day."

Don, who'd been laughing through the entire exchange said, "That's my Pen. Those things are always getting in her way."

I guess there are worse ways to be remembered, but I'd rather have had none of it. I think it was the single worst experience of my life. There was nothing funny about this day.

Chapter 43

The End of Independence

Don's parents arrived early evening and got a suite across the hall from me. I was happy to have the moral support, but I was ready to ship them home if it became too tough for them to deal with. When I got back to the hotel the room was still in shambles, furniture overturned, beds unmade, food everywhere. I had even called the hotel earlier and they reported a clean room. Don's socks still lay right where he collapsed. He must have been putting them on at the time.

Enough with this day. I shut my eyes, walked through the mine field and found the bed.

At 11:30 PM. the nurse called me. Don was still scheduled for a biopsy in the morning, but the nurse said there was no telling when or what would happen. Dr. Freid was still in surgery and Don was really doped up on steroids, still having tremors. The bottom line: "Don't rush over in the morning."

Well, there's no release in the world like sleep, and it was time I had some. Too bad it didn't last long. It had been 2:30 AM when I went to bed. But reality was infiltrating my most beloved of places, my dreams, and at 4:45 AM, life slapped me awake.

This was it. Never the same again.

My future, Don's future was staring me down with its jaundiced, veiny eyes, sunken deep within their sockets. They had no fair tale to tell, that was for sure. I called Don's nurse.

"He's sitting up in a chair. He has the halo on for biopsy, but he has to get an MRI first. He's still pretty dopey, but funny."

I called Don's room.

"The halo hurts a lot; the screws feel like their jamming into my brain, but I feel a lot better than yesterday. I'm so sorry I made you go through that. Are you alright?"

"Yeah, I'm okay. Hey, remember when I told you I was afraid I'd be bored while we were here? Well, you sure took care of that. I owe you one."

Don laughed. "Little bits are coming back to me. It seems like it was really bad."

"No problem. Piece of cake."

After eighteen years of for better or worse, I know he appreciated me saying that, even if it were the furthest thing from the truth.

About midmorning one of Dr. Fried's doctors came in to tell us that they were going ahead with the biopsy as planned, that grand mals were passé (my words) and if they happened again, to call 911 and Dr. Freid. A bit later they whisked Don away, leaving me to drift, alone with my thoughts on a thunder cloud of fear.

About mid-afternoon Don was back. He said the one needle they used to sedate the brain hurt a lot, but nothing else which was pretty amazing because rumor had it the process was pretty painful. Dr. Freid thought he'd only had seizure activity, no stroke. Don was to rest for six hours and then they'd decide if he could be discharged.

Of course, there'd been a glitch – the bit with the drill. Apparently, it went dead halfway through the procedure so Dr. Allan had to pull it out, change the batteries and stick it back into Don's brain. Can you imagine?

After a couple hours, Don was in agony with a pounding headache. He said it felt like they were tightening the screws when they were removing them. They wouldn't give him anything for the pain, wouldn't let him eat, and he was freaking from the steroids. Poor Don. I gave him something, against doctor's orders, because I couldn't stand to see him suffer (ssshhh – our secret!).

Later I went down to the cafeteria – a girl's gotta eat – and I saw the paramedic from the day before. After ascertaining that he remembered me, I told him I might be alone in the suite tonight and would be available to flash him later. (Does that count as a pick up line?) He said, "It's a date." Okay, so I'm having a fantasy moment. Forgive me. Back to reality.....

Truthfully, he said, "Hey, how ya doing today? Anything I can get you?" I said no, thank you, but when I left I said, "Flash you later." He laughed.

Choose the version you like best.

I'm off to the convenience store to buy Dr. Allan more batteries.

Chapter 44

The Race Is On

The next day, July 2nd – ah yes, another major holiday in the hospital – we were making the best of the worst, clowning around to bypass the tedium of hospital hours, which, like prison hours, are on average, thirty-seven minutes longer per hour than those spent in the relative freedom of the outside world. We cracked jokes and made light; Don's dad and I even had a race. I took the elevator, he took the stairs. I won.

But then Dr. Allan came in and told us the devastating news. "The tumors have infiltrated your entire brain. It's the same tumor gone ballistic just like Dr. June said. They're still small, so who knows how much time you have, but there's nothing we can do to help you surgically."

I just stared at him, mouth agape. He looked uncomfortable, but continued.

"If we could freeze things like they are today you would be okay – but we can't. They're growing as we speak. But it's not over just yet. That's the best worst news I can give you. I'm discharging you tonight with higher doses of anti-seizure meds. Let's hope Dr. Harry can find something to buy you time."

I lost it right in front of him, sobbing, out of control, shaking all over. I could care less who was in the room. It was like Chad relapsing all over again although this time there wasn't a smidgen of hope, not a single ray of light, no magic bullet. I was alone, adrift on my own little personal floatation device and not a shoreline in sight. Even Dr. Harry's words held no comfort.

"Don't tell the children until we get the hard pathology. We have weapons to fight it, but it's very bad. Still, don't pick a plot yet. I'm not sending you out to die; I'm sending you out to live. I just don't know how long yet."

Don thanked him and hugged him and then Dr. Harry turned to me:

"I wish you could stop crying until I call you and tell you 'now you can really cry'. I do have things to buy him some time."

I cried harder than the first time. So much for all those little prayers. Now let's pray he doesn't suffer. They should have just let him go yesterday.

Why did they save him if he's only going to deteriorate? I wished I was the one who was dying.

After receiving the news, Don asked me to lay low before I alerted the media. He didn't want to field calls from tons of well-wishing friends and family asking how he was doing and telling him to keep the faith; it was just too exhausting – a selfish move, maybe, but necessary to maintain sanity. Meanwhile, Don's parents were unbelievable, doing everything. While I sat in the hall and cried, Don's dad dressed him and put his clothes and shoes on him. His mom helped him in the bathroom.

Yet all Don could think about was me and how I would be. His parents got hold of me in the hall and told me to chill. "Listen to what Dr. Harry said. He'll hit it with everything he has to buy you time. Not a cure, but time with the kids," his dad said. "It's not over yet," his mom said.

Don said, "It's scary, but it's liberating. The pressure is off. I do what they tell me now. I know the disease, the diagnosis, the prognosis and hope to buy as much quality time as I can. When it becomes too bad, I'll take care of it. I promise."

The race was on.

In my state of hopelessness I couldn't hear a word they were saying.

Chapter 45

Make Mine a Chai-Lite

We were back from Duke and ready to celebrate Fourth of July weekend out of the hospital for a change. We had tons of family in town. I made a huge BBQ on the 4th, steak, chicken, burgers with all the fixin's, side dishes. I went food shopping, did three loads of laundry, went to the swim club, tried to enjoy myself. Don had been erratic, weak, tired all day. I lied down in Chad's room and cried myself to sleep. Fifteen minutes later my mom came in and sat on the bed, rubbed my head, asked me how she could help. I cried harder.

"I either want a boyfriend or to jump off a bridge. Which do you think is safer?" I asked. "I don't know any willing and able men, though. Maybe the bridge would be better. Except it wouldn't feel as good."

"At least you wouldn't have the guilt," Mom replied.

I would've laughed if I wasn't so sad, hurt, pissed, angry, cheated and frustrated. I wanted someone to make me smile, to wine and dine me, to make me feel alive. Someone to take care of my needs for a change. I didn't know the man in this body. He wasn't my type. Not funny, or manly, or spontaneous anymore unless grand mal seizures count for excitement.
I hated this. They should have let him die the other day.

And now he wanted me to sleep with him.
I couldn't. I just couldn't.

At 8:30 PM everyone but Don and I left for the fireworks. I was way too tired and sad to go. Don was just sitting in a chair like a zombie. I said, "I'm taking a bubble bath and going to bed in Chad's room." (Chad was sleeping at my parents.)

"No. I want you to sleep in bed with me. I'm afraid to be alone. I need you to sleep with me."

Thank God eyes don't make any noise because mine were screaming: *NO. I DON'T WANT TO!* I didn't want to listen to him breathe and be afraid he might not. I didn't want him to touch my leg while he was sleeping, to feel him right next to me, this man I no longer knew, whose smell I didn't recognize, now so rancid and stale from all the medication, whose touch felt like sandpaper and made my skin prickle.

This was not the man I fell in love with and if it can't be him then I'm not sleeping in that bed.

During the day I had rubbed his shoulders, held his hand, called him babe, hugged him, but I felt like these gestures were as easily transferable to the kids or the dog. It was an affectionate action, but not a lovey dovey one. I never had that platonic feeling toward him before. I wanted my husband back, healthy, strong, sexy, not this mook with a simple look on his face. God was punishing me for feeling this way, I knew it. That's why it was so painful.

In Hebrew, Chai means life. It was Chad's Hebrew name. But there was very little Chai in the life of a gbm patient, even less for their caretakers and loved ones, like Chai-lite, or maybe even Chai-less. I knew it wasn't his fault, that Don would have never chosen to be sick. I knew he'd want to watch his kids grow, feel good, get old with me. I loved him very much, but the suffering was killing us all.

Bang. Happy 4th of July.

Chapter 46

Don Got Duked

Five days later, Dr. Allan called Don and told him the hard and final results of the biopsy. The one that Dr. Harry asked me to hold off my tears for.

"It's a malignant tumor throughout the entire brain."

Dr. Allan said Dr. Harry would be calling either that night or the next day with a plan of action which may include a flight back to Duke for chemo or staying put for oral meds. That's it. End of conversation.

Meanwhile, Don was getting a bit stronger every day, a little more physical, lasting a bit longer so the whole thing seemed very surreal – we had become characters in a Salvador Dali painting. Don still had total amnesia about the seizures, but he looked great, tanned and healthy. If he wasn't bald you wouldn't suspect there was anything wrong. Some days he worked on the lawn, nothing too strenuous, and had been spending lots of time with the kids, playing games or watching movies, attempting to perform magic with Chad. I didn't leave him alone at all. Don and Chad were working on a new magic show to perform for Chad's gigs. Faith and Don were working on her dollhouse. Between Faith, Chad, my parents or me, someone was always with him. He ran errands with me and was funny, great company. He started going to lunch with friends and patients, having dinner out with family, reconnecting after his disconnect of the last few weeks. Uncle Mel and Aunt Val brought him a wheelchair from their pharmacy. He's not ready for it full time, but we have it for the long hauls. His attitude is amazing and he feels Dr. Harry can buy him some quality time.

"It's all I can hope for, Pen. If there isn't quality time, I don't want to wait. There are no guarantees. I'm just trying to enjoy each day."

His parents were surprised at how well he was taking it. The kids understood now, too, about the time, and not knowing how much of it there was, although it was hard.

When Chad and I were stepping out for a little walk, Chad remarked to his dad, "Don't die on us while we're gone, Daddy." Outside I asked him why he said that. He replied,

"I don't want him to die on me. I don't want to be the one he's left alone with when he keels over."
I tried to explain the chances of that happening were slim and that no matter what happened, it wouldn't be his fault, that it was all out of our hands. Poor guy. After as many deaths as he'd seen, what was surprising was how brave he was being.

Chapter 46

When the Going Gets Tough, Penny Goes Shopping

I love to shop. More importantly, I never met a stress that couldn't be cured by a good shopping spree. Put Faith and me together and we could go for day's straight, stopping only for necessary sustenance and the occasional bathroom break. It's like that saying: "Just let me go shopping and no one gets hurt."

Needless to say, the last nine years were not that great for me, shopping-wise. Yeah, I managed to get out and buy clothes and what not, when faced with the prospect of holey underwear and shredded socks, but now the bigger things were starting to go and it was time to do something about it.

"Pen, it's your house and you have to like what you have in it. Right now, everything you have is at least eight years old, is worn, torn, or has vomit on it," Don said. "Go for it."

That was all I needed. Laura picked me up and off we went. When I found something I loved I checked in on Don. He and Chad and Chris, Chad's friend, were playing a game.

"Take your time, Pen." I felt like I was on a vacation; everyone seemed to behaving a great day.

The magic continued into the evening. We had plans to go out, but our friends bagged. Don said he was feeling too good not to see people so we called other friends and went to an Italian restaurant owned by a patient of Don's. She emailed me the next day, telling me how great it was to see Don doing so well.

It's nice to catch a break once in awhile.

Chapter 47

Swelling, Seizures and Such

July 18, 1999. I told everyone I saw that night that something was up. Don was even quieter than usual – quick with a witty retort if you engaged him, but otherwise he just sat there with the same blank look, his head drooping a little to the side. After two hours, Laura and I went in the pool, and then to a movie, but Rob and Marcia never left his side. I picked Don up from our friends and we arrived home around 10:30 p.m., and Don turned on the television, static, no channel. After a few minutes I asked…

"Why are you watching static?" I asked.

"Oh. I was wondering when it was going to come on."

I switched to a real channel, left him watching and went to bed. When I woke at 3 AM, I found him noticeably absent. He was still in front of the T.V., watching the fuzz since the channel signed off for the night, with the same expression on his face that he had hours earlier.

Oh geez. Focal Seizure. I helped him to bed and at 6:30 AM, he got up and went in the shower.

"Where are you going, Don?"

"The airport."

"Oh, you're going to ride with me to take my sister to the plane?"

"Yeah. I just want to finish my shower."

I left the bedroom to get some things ready and at 7:05 AM returned to find him still in the shower. "Don, come on out. You've been in there for thirty-five minutes."

"I need to shave."

"You just did last night. You look great. We've got to leave in half an hour."

"I have to shave. It won't take long."

I huffed at him, exasperated, and left him to his devices. At 7:30 AM I went back and he was still shaving. I took the razor and he started stacking up his pills real high.

"Don!" Admittedly, I may have shrieked. "What are you doing?"

"Getting ready for the trip."

"We're only going to the airport. You don't need anything. Get your shoes and get in the car."

I left, came back ten minutes later and every article of clothing he owned was arranged in neat piles on the bed. He was packing.

"Don, we aren't going to North Carolina today. We're taking Susan to the airport."

"And then we catch our plane."

"On Tuesday. Today is Sunday."

"I don't want to be late."

"You won't be. Get in the car." I finished dressing him and hustled him out the door. On the way there he said, "I'm very confused today, huh?" Then he opened the window at least fifteen times, put his fingers in his mouth and threw out his gum, over and over, window up, window down, window up, window down, until finally Chad said, "Daddy, what are you doing?" and Don said, "Spitting out my gum," and Chad said, "You haven't been chewing any gum."

Then Don said he had a premonition that we went to Denny's Restaurant so we did and Don ordered a "bacon sausage and cheese omelets, my favorite.

"He doesn't eat that," I told the poor girl. "He keeps kosher. Just bring him two pancakes."

"Daddy, why are you so confused today?" Chad asked.

"What do you mean? I love bacon."

"You've never had a piece of bacon in your life," I quipped. Maybe it was that comment, but he suddenly snapped out of it, back to normal, confusion gone in a poof. When we got home, though, Chad said he wanted to hide somewhere.

"He's not acting like Daddy."

So my parents came and took the kids. Later that night, Don told me he hears things in his head, swooshing, that the patch from the incision of the port itches very badly and that he can't lift his hand over his shoulder. Other than that, he was fine, he said, and went off to nap.

Aaaggggghhhhhh. Not a good day.

7:30 PM. Same crap, same day. Don woke from a nap panicked and told me not to leave his side, that his head was swooshing again, that he felt strange. He had me come into the bathroom with him when he had to go, then he started brushing his teeth and wouldn't stop. Fifteen minutes later I took the toothbrush out of his hand and he turned on the shower to which I protested.

"I take them every morning."

"It's night. Come eat dinner."

8:45 PM. "Don, do you know who the President is?"

"Same schmuck it was the last time you asked. And I even know the difference between real sex and oral sex. I think I know more who the President is than

Bill does. But I feel weird, Pen. Like I've slept for days. Don't leave me."

Same crap, next day. I was so tired, I had to go to bed, but Don didn't want me to leave him so we agreed that he'd lie down and not get out of bed no matter what. But throughout the night, time and again, I was jolted awake to find Don in the other room, staring at himself in the mirror.

"You can't do this, Don. It's the middle of the night. I need to sleep."

"I'm not trying, Pen. It's just that I'm confused."

"Do you know who the schmucky President is?"

"Yes."

"And do you know who I am?"

"My schmucky wife."

We both laughed.

"My ship may be sinking, Pen, but I'm gonna leave you laughing if it's the last thing I do."

Later that same day . . . *Oy oy oy* . . .

Don went to be about 3:00 PM and at 4:00 PM he was due for his anti-seizure meds, but I figured it could wait until he woke up. Big mistake. At 6:30 PM I woke him up and made him take the pills – no easy feat – and asked him to get up and have dinner.

"Why would I eat dinner so early in the morning, Pen?"

"It's night."

"Stop playing with me, Pen. I'm having a hard enough time."

Chad came in and helped me lift him – Don couldn't do it on his own – and together we dressed him; Chad put on his socks and I put on his pants.

"I know," I said. "Let's play 'Follow the Leader.' Me first, then you, then Chad." That's me, always chipper.

"Okay."

Yeah right. When I turned around he wasn't there. He'd stopped at the bathroom to brush his teeth, "because it's morning, Pen. I have to." I just let him.

I gave him veal for dinner. He asked for his bagel so I toasted one and put it on the same plate as his dinner. I had to cut everything up for him because he'd lost strength in his right hand. He ate it all, but before he did he played with it, making swirling designs on the plate and arranging it in circles.

Faith's asking tons of questions. Chad's quiet, just helping when he can. Don's mom called and cried. A friend called and cried. No time now for me. I understand what all the people on the brain tumor list meant when they said you don't cry. It just doesn't fit in the schedule of doing what you have to do.

Dr. Freid called about our plans to fly back to North Carolina – he's offered to help. It'll be like flying with an infant minus the diapers, wipes and car seat.

Chapter 48

I Need You to Huff and Puff

July 20, 1999. We were back at Duke so Don could try out this new protocol. He hadn't been right since he'd been admitted locally to have a port inserted in his brain, but Dr. Freid refused to give him steroids since it would ruin his chances to qualify.

So much for Dr. Freid's advice. By the time we got to Duke, Don was so dehydrated he couldn't even pee. First the nurse couldn't find a vein. Then no urine sample and finally, he failed the pulmonary function test.

"Does Dr. Freid know he's acting like this?" his nurse asked.

"Yep."

"How tall are you, Dr. Juros?"

"Five foot."

"Five foot what?"

"Five foot even."

She refrained from laughing, but the stress of it was tugging at her, too. "I need you to blow into this tube as hard as you can, Dr. Juros. Huff and puff."

"Then put my wife in front of me naked." The other nurses were laughing. "She'll make sure I die with a smile on my face. That's her goal."

Don's nurse started crying.

Don quit while he was ahead. He'd failed the protocols and the nurse said he needed steroids to treat the complex partial seizure, exactly what I'd been begging Dr. Freid for all week.

I wish I could say I took the news calmly. They sent us home early with instructions to hydrate locally. *Drink globally. Hydrate locally.*

Chapter 49

If Words Could Make Wishes Come True

I brought Don home from Duke, propped him up in our bed and gathered Faith and Chad around him. I asked him his dying wishes. Without a second thought he replied:

"That's easy. For Faith," Don said, taking her hand, "you don't have to go to Rutgers University but I'd like you to seriously consider it. For me Rutgers was the best time of my life. I had no worries, was playing the best tennis of my life, and had your Mom with me every weekend, I only have fond memories of my time at Rutgers. I'd also like you to establish the Dr. Don Juros Memorial Tennis Scholarship in my name at your high school. Only not until you graduate. And don't involve Mommy, she'll be busy enough. Ask Memom if she can help you establish a scholarship for a graduating girl and boy who would like to pursue their tennis in college and who love the sport like you and I do. This way I'll feel like a piece of me got you through high school and college. After that you're on your own."

A few weeks later Don did take Faith to visit his Alma Mater, Rutgers College in Piscataway, New Jersey. He showed her his dorms, the science labs and food courts. He was in a wheelchair, but he was able to share with her the joy college had brought to him.

"Chad, for you my dying wish is that you be considered cured from your cancer, and that you spread the magic all over the world. Maybe everyone can find the magic in their lives like we did." The three of us were crying; Don was so explicit, so precise.

"And for you, Pen, my wifey for lifey," he said, holding my hand and, wiping away my tears, "it's really very simple. My wish for you is to bury me and go out there and find someone who will make you smile, make you laugh, love you and appreciate you the way I did. But whatever you do, don't settle. And I'd like for you to publish your book. Maybe from you're sharing of our pain and magical moments you will help bring strength to someone else." That was Don – always thinking of others.

"I didn't ask you you're dying wishes for us," I said. "I asked you if you had any dying wishes. Wishes for you that maybe we make come true."

"That's easy, Pen. I'd like to be at Chad's bar mitzvah," he said.

"You know Chad's only 11. He's got two years yet. Most likely you aren't going to make it baby." "Figure it out, Pen. You moved mountains up at CHOP. You can figure something out." "Don, I might be able to talk the talk with a few doctors, but I'm not powerful enough to change Jewish law, Jewish tradition."

"Yes you are."

And sure enough, I was. I called my Rabbis, asked if it were possible. It was unheard of; being bar mitzvah'd two years early. I told them I didn't need their blessing but would love to have it. Miraculously, they agreed.

Rabbi Krauss said "how can we deny this incredible husband and father his dying wish. Chad will be bar mitzvah'd at age 11."

For the next five weeks we had a healthy focus.

Chapter 50

And It Just Keeps Getting Weirder

Do you know what it's like to have your husband walk around with a half-shaven face? The disease was robbing Don of his mind and his dignity. Faith asked Don if he could live to be eighty like that.

"Possible, but not probable," he said. Chad asked for a promise that Don would be at his wedding.

"I can't promise you anything, Chad."

And so it went those days after we returned from Duke. Faith asked me, "Is what Daddy has terminal?" I said yes, and that we had talked about it before. She said before she didn't know what terminal meant.

"So as we're talking, Daddy's dying? I thought some people lived a year or two."

"They can. We don't know. But it's incurable.

My daughter's voice, shaky and broken: "Did the doctors tell you how long he had?"

"No. They said it wasn't near the end, and they're hoping the chemo buys some time. But you do see a major difference in him."

Her voice rougher now, almost defiant. "Answer me! "Is he dying?"

"No. But he is weaker. That's why we don't want to wait for Chad's bar mitzvah. We don't know how long of a future he has."

Don and Chad listened to the entire thing and Faith didn't ask any more questions.

Finally Don said, "I'm fighting as hard as I can Faith just to spend even one more minute with the three of you."

She wasn't consoled. Nor was Chad who said, "This is so sad. Just put me to bed."

Somebody get me out of July, please. It's as if Don's already died and left me the body to take care of. He came out of the bathroom with hydration tubes coming out of the fly in his pants. I told him he can't walk around like that, he looked like a flasher. He thought that was supremely funny, but tucked them back in all the same. An hour later the doctors took the tubes out. He ran around all day doing

errands with me for the bar mitzvah. He enjoyed that,
but he's slow, hunched over, even his voice is different
because of the steroids. He wants to eat all the time.
I told him he's become the perfect husband,
so agreeable, doing whatever I tell him. So sad.

Chapter 51

Do You Believe in Magic?

On September 6, 1999, two years before the traditional time, Chad was bar mitzvah'd.

There he was, only eleven, on the Bima reading the Torah in front of two hundred and four of our closest friends and family all gathered to celebrate Chad's life with us. I didn't want it to be, couldn't let it be a boring service, so I had friends and family participate on the Bima, reading poems, singing songs, playing the piano, violin and guitar. Rabbi's Krauss and Geller both attended. The only "normal" thing was Chad, reading his Torah portion, but except for that and a few prayers, the rest was tailored to Chad's life. Since Don's father was a cantor, he sang "Those Were the Days My Friend," and "Sunrise, Sunset." Others sang half a dozen more songs like, "You've Got a Friend," and "Bridge Over Troubled Water." When we arrived at Temple Emeth Shalom that morning I put Don in his seat on the bima, placed his tallis around him and basically he just stared for four hours. He seemed to be going in and out of focal seizures. When we needed him to stand to do the Tallit Ceremony over Chad, his best friend since diapers, Howard Freedman, helped me hold him up.

I gave a speech. Me, who gets nervous with any kind of public display, gave an honest-to-God speech during which I never looked up the entire time for fear I'd break down. I told my story and thanked the world – at least that part of it that had helped us so much – our family and friends. They kept me loving and laughing through all this tsouris (pain) and were there everyday to remind us of the pleasurable side of life. They helped me to laugh through my tears with their generosity of spirit. Laughter – that's what kept me going. The speech lasted thirty-seven minutes and by the time I was done there wasn't a dry eye in the place.

Don made a nice quick speech about his own bar mitzvah, but he had a tough time getting through it and had to take long breaks. No one rushed him though. They knew he'd never have this opportunity again. Howard brought Don's own yalmulkes from his bar mitzvah that was 27 years earlier, he had kept a bunch of them in his attic all these years, go figure, and passed them out to the immediate family. Faith helped Chad with the Hebrew. Another group effort. Everyone told me how thin I looked, how radiant, that Don and I were an inspiration. I sat back and enjoyed the sights and sounds and just kvelled. Amazingly, throughout the fiendish roller coaster ride of the last decade, Don and I had managed to raise two great kids.

At the reception, Don hung in there for the important traditional rituals. He stood and clapped while we all did the hora (circle dance) and allowed himself to be lifted on the chair, but he didn't push himself to join in. He danced to "Mac the Knife" with Chad and "Just You and Me" with me, and a James Taylor song with Faith. Chad and I danced to "I'll Be There," our song. Faith and I danced to our song, "My Girl" by the Temptations. We had a magician entertaining the tables, a DJ on stilts, leading the *Macarena,* the *Electric Slide* and congo lines. Everyone told me I should go into the party-planning business.

Chad jumped out of a magician's box for the formal introductions. It's a tradition for the Bar mitzvah, in this case, Chad, to place a candle in the cake for each person who's been an inspiration in their lives or had a profound effect of some sort. The Bar Mitzvah says something, a word of gratitude or praise for that person's guidance and then the individual comes forward and lights his or her candle. Chad had so many people to thank his cake looked like a towering inferno. When Dr. Wasserman, Chad's oncologist came forward, he got a standing ovation. Another magical moment. Once the candles were lit I took Don to one of the hotel rooms in the building and put him to bed. I hear the video is very nice but I refuse to watch and have never looked at the pictures either.

Later, Don remarked that he never kissed so many men in his entire life, more men, he thought, than women.

"Yeah, but did you like it more?" I asked. "That's all I need to worry about."

Not a single thing went wrong: food, centerpieces, DJ, weather, guests, all perfect. So fairy tales do exist and dreams really do come true. I wish the spell would have never been broken.

Don and I flew to Duke the next morning. By night he'd be receiving an MRI and if the results were good, chemo the next day.

And despite the inevitable, Don was still so positive. "Isn't it wonderful the way we mix the happiness of our kids' bat and bar mitzvah's with all the sadness in our lives? It's the highs and lows, the way life really is, Pen." And he meant it.

I had said to him driving home from radiation one day, "You know, Don, life really stinks," and he said, "No, it doesn't, Penny. Life is great. It's the dying that stinks."

La Chaim. To Life.

Chapter 52

The Beginning of the End

September 22, 1999. Don had his appointment with Dr. June today, the neurosurgeon at HUP who performed his total resection eleven months ago. The appointment was originally scheduled last June, before the eleven grand mal seizures and the cardiac arrest at Duke, before the biopsy, before the news that the tumors had spread like oil on water, growing ever more dangerous by the day. Duke told us there was no reason to keep this appointment, but Don always admired and respected Dr. June and wanted his opinion as well as to ask some questions. Don also wanted to talk to Linda Stevens, the social worker, because of her wonderful way of putting things into perspective. Everything she'd told him in the past had proved to be necessary and important.

A few minutes after we signed in, Dr. June's secretary came to us and very kindly explained that Dr. June had just looked at Don's MRI's and although he was still willing to speak with Don, he wanted him to understand that there was nothing Dr. June or anyone else could do for him.

"I know the tumors are inoperable. I just want to keep the appointment."

"No problem. As long as you know what you're facing when you walk in that room."

"In the past, every single encounter Don had with Dr. June started with, "How's your tennis game going?" Not this time though.

"Has anyone told you how bad your MRI is?"

"We were told the tumors had all grown twenty-five percent, but I couldn't ask questions then. Now I'm ready," Don said.

Dr. June put the scans on the wall and I almost passed out. My head throbbed and I swayed in my seat. Don grabbed me before I fell.

"Maybe you're not ready to hear this, Penny," Dr. June said. "You can wait out in the hall or even sit down and have only Don take a look."

"I'm just in shock is all," I replied. "I want to see and hear."

"Okay – Don has extra large tumors all growing in the frontal lobes. His original tumor that was fully resected was in the left frontal lobe. The right frontal lobe is just one big tumor now. There's another larger one next to it and two more tumors in the left, about three centimeters each, which is big for their location. The edema is shocking. It looks like a massive cloud in the sky."

Then he moved to the back of the brain and showed us a series of tumors close to the motor strip, all around one centimeter, but with swelling around them, too.

"When I diagnosed you I told you that you probably had about a year to eighteen months to live. Next month is a year. My diagnosis hasn't changed and that's only if the new chemo works. If not, you have even less time. Of course, no one can know, but from looking at your MRI, that's my best-educated medical guess. There's no more to be done surgically – there are too many lesions for us to operate. My hope for you at this point is that you die from the pressure and swelling of the frontal lobe tumors before the back tumors grow too large. If they do, they'll hit your motor strip and you'll be paralyzed or have a stroke or go into a coma and linger longer. I'm sorry."

Don said, "You've always been right on the money with my diagnosis. Tell me what it will be like."

"Don't attempt to wean yourself off of the steroids, no matter the side effects. You need every bit of them to keep the swelling down. If your November MRI at Duke proves the new chemo is working then you can wean yourself, but I don't know if that's an appointment you'll make. In time, the steroids won't work anymore and the confusion will set in."

Don took the news complacently, resigned, not like a man who'd just been given the death sentence. I on the other hand was struggling for what meager breaths I could capture and even then, I didn't utilize them, sending them deep down into my lungs to be distributed as life-giving oxygen throughout the body, but rather held them there captive, as if to keep the life force from escaping. But it doesn't work that way, does it? It's only in the release that we're free to draw the next one, and neither Don nor I knew how to do that.

All the confusion of the previous weeks, Don forgetting how to use a telephone, not knowing what the number six looked like, taking three hours in the bathroom and half a day to shave a quarter of his face, these were all just small tastes of what the future would be.

"I'll be there to help you any way I can, to make you more comfortable" Dr. June said, "but there's honestly nothing anyone can do for you."

Maybe it was because I'd been holding my breath, but at this point, my brain reminded me it was still in my head, pounding to get out, to be released from the knowledge of all it had learned in the last fifteen minutes. My eyes were in strobe mode, pulsating along with the pain. A migraine, perhaps?

Still, no time to deal with it. Linda Stevens was waiting for us, Dr. June said, and she shook our hands just as my beeper went off. I was desperate for two Tylenol and a minute alone with my husband to talk about what we'd just heard, but Faith was beeping and Linda was waiting.

When I hung up, Linda gave us a very powerful, very pertinent talk. How I took notes with my head pounding and my eyes watering and nausea settling in for a nice cozy weekend stay in my stomach, I don't know. Don seemed fine, just quieter than usual and, as always, more concerned for me than himself.

Linda said that when they sat down to give us the death sentence a year ago, they were impressed by our support system – both sets of parents were present – and it would be that support system that would get us through this. She also said she saw in Don and me a total commitment to each other and our family.

"You entered the room holding hands, something we don't see much of, and you held hands the entire time. And when Dr. June told you that you were dying, Don, the first thing you both said at the exact same time was (and I was able to say this with her because I remembered it perfectly) 'what about the children?' That was remarkable. Almost every patient says something like, 'no way, can't be, oh my God, why? how? when?' etc., but not you guys. You immediately thought of Chad and Faith and that was amazing to us. Neither one of you cried that day. Instead, Penny said, 'No one leaves this room until we make a decision about how we're going to tell Faith and Chad.' Don, right then we knew your family would be okay."

She went on to talk about how much effort Don had made into squeezing the last bits of quality time out and that it was likely his healthy lifestyle and take charge attitude that got him to this point.

Don interjected: "But what about Penny? Why isn't she more distraught like my brother and my parents? She's lived with cancer for eight years now and she still finds reasons to smile and tell jokes?"

"Did either of you notice what happened ten minutes ago?" Linda asked. "Penny was in a state of shock, staring at the MRI, and hearing from Dr. June that there was no more he could do for the man she loved and what happened? Before she could even take it all in, her beeper went off. That's why, guys. Penny's busy. She doesn't have time to be depressed or react. And right now that's a blessing. She can't stay in bed and cry, no matter how badly she may want to. She can't have a nervous breakdown. She's made her family her first priority as have you, Don. Penny will make sure your kids are taken care of because you took care of Penny. You never were in denial. You did all you could to make the last bit of time memorable for the kids. You sold the office, you accepted your diagnosis and you have no unfinished business. If you died tomorrow, you'd be at peace because all your plans are in place. Most spouses ignore it, hoping it will go away. But you looked each other in the eye while making funeral plans. You've given your family a gift." She stopped to take a breath and give us a chance to catch up.

"Tell me what death will be like," Don said, and right then my beeper went off. We all laughed.

"Answer that, Penny, while I talk to Don about death."

"Don't you dare say a word. I want to hear this, too." I called the kids and dealt with their needs, then went back to our conversation.

She said Don would get super tired, a tired like you couldn't believe, and if the front tumors got him, he'd die peacefully, and if the back tumors got him, he'd die confused. The brain would swell so much it would just burst. He could go into a coma, but he wouldn't feel frustrated or unhappy because he just wouldn't know what was happening. A major seizure or a heart attack would be a gift. It would soon be time to get me a barf bag, but thankfully, she changed topics.

Linda asked Don if he had any other concerns.

"I'm so happy and at peace with all my relationships. That's the beauty of being told you're going to die. You have time to plan. I would like to take one more trip, but the idea of packing a suitcase is even exhausting. So I'll enjoy the kids from home."

"That's it?" Linda asked. "No other worries?"

Don closed his eyes for a few moments and his face looked so intense as if he were in a great deal of pain. "Linda, it would kill me right now, I would just die from the pain if Chad were to relapse again. I have to die knowing he made it all the way."

"You know what, Don? I hope your worry never happens – and you die in your sleep."

Chapter 53

Post Traumatic Stress Syndrome

October 5, 1999. And I wonder sometimes why I get the shakes.

While Chad and I were at his sixteen-month hospital exam, we came home to some really weird post-trauma experiences, like Vietnam Vets, but without the gunfire reverb. Apparently it's very common. But just like a Vet who reacts to a car backfiring as if he's in combat, Chad heard the clanging of a church bell or any kind of little dings and would start screaming, "Oh my God, not again. Stop the noise." He thought it was the IV pole that held his chemo going off. If I would hear any overhead paging, crying in the middle of the night or ambulance sounds, I'd just need to sit for a few minutes and work my way through the flashback of bundling him up, no matter day or night, throwing him in the back of the car, and racing off to the nearest hospital. The truth is, having performed this little maneuver well over sixty times in a year; the steps were hard-wired and second nature, like brushing my teeth.

So why am I reliving it now? Because after midnight I heard a noise, almost mouse-like in nature, but it turned out to be Chad moaning for me and immediately I was back in time. I screamed for Don who came running despite his inability to do anything quickly these days. We found Chad in his room, curled up in a ball, clutching his stomach, the pain evident on his face. I felt his head and pulled off his clothes to give him breathing room while Don packed a suitcase. One touch and I knew he didn't have a fever.

"No. Stop. He's okay. Look how crazy we get, Don. He doesn't have a fever. He's fine. I'll get in bed with him and you go to sleep."

It took two hours of me rubbing Chad's back and belly, whispering the mantra I used during the long days and horribly long nights: "You will not be sick. You will be well. You will be well. You are doing so well. You will be the miracle."

At 3 AM, my heart rate returned to a more regular clip and Chad was starting to feel a bit better. Finally, we both fell asleep. I got up at 6 AM, gave the kids breakfast and put them on the bus while the memory of the night before floated around the ethers of my grey matter for awhile.

It didn't help that for the past week Chad had been coming home upset. The kids had been calling him "cancer boy," and "chemo kid", saying that he had it twice already and now his dad had brain cancer. No one wanted to sit near him because they thought the disease he had was contagious. Two boys actually gave him swirleys. Swirleys is when someone holds your head down in the toilet as someone else flushes. Yikes. The poor kid. Don and I talked to Chad's teacher who made announcements, but fear breeds cruelty and the fact is, there's nothing we can do for him, but help toughen him up. It would be easier if he wasn't so sensitive, but that's what makes him so special. Don tried role playing with him, but that left him hysterical so I sent Don away while I pried the reason for this crying jag out of Chad.

"Daddy said that I was his hero, Mom. I can't believe it. He said because I was so strong he wanted to be strong like me."

Oy. There goes my heart again. I can hear the fibers snapping as it pulls itself with an excruciating slowness up my esophagus then wedges in the back of my throat. *Oh good. A sensation I recognize.*

As if I didn't have enough to angst about my birthday was coming. I always start in with the extra worry around that time, holding my breath, scared what might happen on this year's date.

Chapter 54

Life's a Beach OR Reality Sucks

I'm fearful that my birthday present this year will be someone deciding to die. That someone could be my husband. His seizure levels were thirty percent higher than the levels that make doctors raise eyebrows and fidget with the dials on their X-ray machines. Dr. Freid was more than a little concerned and wanted us on a plane to North Carolina, a position he backed off of when I told him Don was in Mr. Man Mode, fixing things around the house and flashing a left-brain adeptness that belies his condition. Other than perpetual tiredness, you'd never know he had a single mutant cell in his brain.

Then again, it could be my Poppop who did the dying. Unlike Don, he'd lived a long healthy life up to eighty-six, and was married to the woman he loved for sixty-five of them. I was taking bets with myself about who was going to go first – Don, Poppop, or me from a shredded aorta.

Sure enough Poppop died on October 22, the day after my birthday. Mommom called me that morning crying. She said she wanted so badly for nothing to happen to me during my birthday week. I replied "nothing did happen, finally it was a quiet day" and that's when she shared with me that I was the first to know. A week later I was a mess at the service, watching Don's father direct it while his son lay in a hospital bed. There were about a hundred people there. My grandfather's ashes were buried next to my grandmother's sisters and brothers, some of which were still alive, but they have this huge section reserved for their family so he'll be surrounded with love. My grandmother, bless her heart, brought Poppop's ashes from Arizona wrapped in Christmas paper. It was enough that he was cremated for a Jewish burial, but Christmas paper? *Oy.*

Chad's school situation is better, thank God, with the help of his guidance counselor. Don said the other day he feels like he could make it to the kids graduation – Faith's is five years away – and the physical therapist was amazed at how much stronger he was since the last visit and said he wanted to see Don on the tennis court again. Don's latest dream was to die on the court, making the perfect shot. Combining dreams and death in the same fantasy seems like an oxymoron to me. I never said anything when he made those kinds of pronouncements.

Faith was happy with eighth grade, loved her classes, friends, teachers. Both the kids got very upset when they saw Don tremoring and sleeping in front of the T.V. so readily. Together, they'd help him in and out of the car and push him in the wheelchair; together they watched him deteriorate.

I mentioned to Faith that when Chad was thirteen, I'd like to go to Israel.

"Daddy should be better by then, she replied. "Or he can stay with Grandma Janet." Both kids knew the truth, but didn't want to go there yet, so they were planning out, filling in with vague brush strokes the shape and tint and hue of a future without their father. I guess they were reassuring themselves that life goes on. It was maybe not the most accurate scenario they could imagine, but it was a scenario and not a black hole.

Uncle Mel and Aunt Valerie were participating in a twenty-six mile walk on the Atlantic City Boardwalk to benefit leukemia. We intended to get Don to the finish line in time to cheer them on. Don's sister and her family were coming for the weekend, a balm for Don's spirit, and we had tons of activities planned.

I ordered new carpet – "Raspberry Tart." It looked great against the couch.

"Just in time for a Shiva," Don said.

I didn't go to sleep until 3:30 AM and at four, Don woke up with a lot of muscle pain, mostly in the knees, probably due to the high doses of steroids. There was nothing I could do for him so I took Chad to Hebrew School as I always do on Sunday when no one's in the hospital or dying.

My friend Ellen came up to me and said, "My God, Penny. I haven't seen you since the bar mitzvah. What an eloquent speech. Your voice didn't crack. You didn't cry. How did you do it?"

Now I can usually talk about Don or Chad and what's happening with them by detaching me from the situation like some third-party observer, but the future was closing in on me and the hope I'd nursed in the past, first for Chad and then for Don, was fading like cheap upholstery. I felt my throat closing up, but managed to choke out an answer.

"It's a diversion, Ellen. What else do I have to do, but sit and watch him die?"

"You don't look like you're eating or sleeping. You look like you're in pain. Are you okay?"

"I'm eating better than ever in my life. I lick my Oreos and eat my Tootsie Rolls and watch Don die." Then I walked away. Poor Ellen.

I got in the car and instead of meeting my friend for breakfast, I went to the beach, a seven-minute ride from our house. No husband, no kids, no friends or errands, no obligations.

I climbed the lifeguard stand and just sat. I didn't close my eyes, just melded into the breathtaking, regenerating view before me. The ocean waves lapping endlessly at the shore while the seagulls screeched and cawed and dove for bits of food. The occasional joggers blurred by along with the obligatory sailboat, all to make it picture perfect. The murmur of tourists strolling the boards wafted into my state of semiconsciousness along with the smell of salty ocean air. The drone of a single engine plane flying off in the distance became a mantra.

I propped my purse up behind my head, creating a makeshift pillow and relaxed into the scene. Now I've never been one for visualization, can't say I'd even know how to do it, but I guess that's what happened because suddenly I was slow dancing with a tall, strong, adorable man who wasn't my husband. He had broad shoulders and dreamy eyes as clear as the ocean water, and a fantastic smile. And here's the amazing part. As we danced, I noticed that I wasn't holding him up. Nor was he holding me up. It was wonderful!

This man, this stranger who I'd never seen before was humming, *What a Wonderful World*, by Louis Armstrong, the music vibrating right in my ear, and he was smiling. We both were. And strangest of all, I realized for the first time I wasn't slow dancing with my husband, the only man other than my father with whom I'd ever slow danced. My fantasies were no longer including Don.

I had no idea how much time had passed, no concept of anything happening in my surrounding environ other than my dance with my mystery man, and then – boom. My beeper went off. In a split second, my fantasy dissolved into the sand. I almost wept, "No, no, no...." I wasn't ready to come back from my little vacation, didn't want to face the world as a mom or a wife or a caretaker. I just wanted a few more minutes. I started rationalizing, trying to ignore it, it wasn't my beeper it was — I jumped when it went off again.

Faith was crying, screaming, "Daddy's having a seizure. Come home, Mommy, please."

"Faith, calm down. Do you mean a grand mal?"

She said he was spacey, weird, staring at her and couldn't hear what she was saying or maybe he could, but just acted like he couldn't. I told her to put the phone to his ear.

"Don, can you hear me?"

"Yeah," he said in an alien, unrecognizable voice.

"Don, let Faith put you in bed. Get in the middle and stay there until I can get Chad and get home to you, okay? Do you hear me?"

"Yeah."

"Okay, give Faith back the phone."

I stayed on the phone with her until she got him to bed. I looked at my watch. Forty minutes had passed and for thirty-five of them, I'd been dancing on the beach with a man I'd never met.

Back to reality.

Chapter 55

Wipe It Off The Map

October 27, 1999. Well, we may have made it through the actual day, but we couldn't make it through the week without a crisis. After listening to my husband moan and complain for days on end about the pain – so bad it even reached his pinkies – I called Duke. They asked me to put Don on the phone and what does he do? Pooh pooh the pain. He didn't let on about his inability to sit still, about the incessant heating pads, about popping Tylenol every two hours.

"My wife can't stand to see me in pain so she worries. I can handle it, though."

The nurse asked to speak with me and proceeded to tear me a new one. *Sheesh.* After I hung up I freaked, told Don to go live with someone else for a week and see what level of care he got. The side effects and sleeplessness were getting harder to deal with and instead of a little understanding I get a big tub of ridicule dumped in my lap. Don apologized, realized he was responsible, but the crap is still sitting there right behind the apology, stinking like it's been baking in the sun.

The next morning I awoke to Don hitting me. I couldn't understand it, thought he was just having a bad dream, but once jarred to alertness, I realized Don was having a seizure. The children heard the commotion in their bedrooms and came running. It was 4 AM. Chad came running in first and witnessed Don spaz all over me, while I lied there, trapped under his weight and trying to push him off so I could dial 911. When I got free, I dressed and had Faith and Chad run across the street together and bang on the neighbor's door. Our neighbor came over to watch them until my parents could get home from work. I called them at their jobs and they came running – as always. What with the series of seizures during the ambulance ride to Shore Memorial Hospital – three ambulances, three paramedics, the kids in hysterics, was it a slow ER day, or what? – and Don's little stay in ICU followed by both Rabbis, Geller and Krauss, saying the Mishaberach over him, well, its crap on crap, I tell you. Even Don's feet were in tremor. When he got to the hospital he told the nurse he had things to do around the house. He didn't even realize he was in the hospital.

On a lighter note, my friend, Bill Schmidt sent me a huge box – I'm talking *ginormous* – filled with Tootsie Rolls, and not the mini kind either, but the big, thick suckers. And this after Rabbi Krauss was kind enough to tell me I looked like I dropped a few pounds. Forget that baby. I've got a box of Tootsie Rolls to get me through the night.

Chapter 56

Starting Today

The next day there was no difference in Don. Dr. June beeped me after getting the MRI results and said, "Do you realize, Penny that Don is probably never going to get better? You need to prepare yourself for hospice or nursing care."

It was exactly one year ago today that they'd told us to get our affairs in order, that Don had one year left, and we hadn't missed a step, we got it all in order down to the most minute details. Apparently all that was left was the lingering, miserable death part.

The MRI showed the frontal tumors were much larger and the chemo wasn't working. Neither was Don for that matter. He could barely sit up without assistance. He could eat though. Man, could he eat. The steroids had really amped up his hunger. It was then it hit me. I'd been mourning my husband's loss for the last seven years.

His erratic behavior had started only a few months after Chad's initial diagnosis, but even so, I deferred to him in all things medical. Now I couldn't do it any longer. Starting today I was going to have to make decisions for my husband and how he was going to live until he died which meant choosing between hospital and hospice care. His parents would help me, but ultimately it was my decision. I was finally alone in the world. And overnight I became both father and mother to my children.

Faith had a bad night of crying. We lay on my bed talking about everything. She was concerned that her friends didn't get it. Some were ignoring her and others just thought Don was going to get better.

"Who's going to walk me down the aisle when I get married?"

"I will."

"There's no chance it will be Daddy now. Now I get it."

"Me, too, Faith. Now I get it, too."

Chapter 57

Man's Best Friend

Muffin, the dog we bought Faith to show her unconditional love, was dying of cancer. She was diagnosed with adrenal gland cancer and Don and I were petrified to share the news with Faith. She knew her dog was sick, it was obvious how weak and unresponsive Muffin had become, but she never suspected cancer for her dog, too. The dog wasn't eating much anymore and Don would use an eyedropper to give it water. We knew the time had come to take Muffin to the vet to put her to sleep. Faith was devastated, Chad and Don were sad, I felt bad, but truthfully, had nothing left to give. Just as we dealt with everything else in life, we went as a family to the veterinarian's office. Faith carried the dog; the doctor came in and explained the procedure, gave us a few minutes alone with Muffin to say our good-byes and then came back in the room and took her from Faith's arms.

Faith was incredibly strong; I was surprised. She told

Muffin that she was her best friend, that she was glad we picked her. We all gave Muffin a kiss, we all cried, and we all left, holding hands and each other. Afterwards, we went out to dinner to celebrate Muffin's life.

"Everything or everyone I ever loved, basically, has been diagnosed with cancer except for you and me, Mom," Faith said. "When will it be our time?"

"Never. One can only hope and pray – never."

Chapter 58

How Many More Chapters?

It didn't take a rocket scientist to know that the book of my life with Don was nearing an end. When my sister, Don's mother, and I got to the hospital I knew even before I entered the room that things were no better. His head was hanging to the side funny and he could only answer questions with yes or no answer and even then it took awhile. He needed help getting to the commode. It took two nurses and an orderly to get him to move one step. The oncologist said there were no plans to move him out of ICU until he was stable which might be never. He was better than when he arrived, but only because he was so drugged, and he couldn't get out of ICU until he was off the drugs. Even if they did get him stable, he'd likely go to a sub acute facility which was shorthand for short-term nursing home. No one knew how long he'd live – days or weeks. He maybe had a few good days left, but most of all he was just lingering. If he did come home, he would need an RN, occupational and physical therapy, and round the clock care. The doctors advised against this because of what the kids had already been through plus my insurance only covered twelve hours a day so I'd be the primary caretaker for the other twelve; I couldn't do it alone.

The doctors said that what he was experiencing were mini brain attacks, like a mini heart attack, and the best we could hope for was that he'd have a stroke and not wake up. At that point it was impossible to give him any more chemo or radiation since there was nothing that could be done and until he was stable. They also said I shouldn't bring the kids to see him because he could have a seizure in front of them, or worse, not know who they were.

One of the docs told me that it was so ironic that Don and I met at a dance because we glided through life so gracefully, never stepping on each other's toes and when one was leading the other followed. That made me cry for quite some time. Don's doctor tennis buddies told me no heroics now, keep a copy of his living will on me at all times and just make him comfortable.

Later at home, when the phone rang, I screamed, "Oh, no. This is it." I assumed it would be Don's nurse saying he had a stroke or died or something and when I heard his voice say, "Hi, Babe," I lost it. Don's mom was crying all the time. Me, too, except when I was with the kids.

The time for miracles was over. Now I was just praying for a quick, peaceful death. To my surprise, my husband had other ideas.

Chapter 59

Change of Plans

When Faith came home the first thing I asked was if she wanted to see her father. "Yes," was her immediate response. Don was sitting up in bed when we arrived and when he saw Faith he smiled big and kissed her hand. The nurse told me he had another seizure before we arrived, a "petit mal." She asked to see me in the hall.

The nurse told me that after explaining to Don what DNR means – Do No Resuscitate – Don refused to sign the papers that would release him. I was shocked. Floored. Flabbergasted. After a year of telling me he wouldn't want to live like a vegetable, what happened? I asked the nurse if he was lucid when he said this and she said "perfectly".

I walked back into the room and watched him watching me through shaded eyes, like a fox. I put up my dukes like I was going to box him.

"I know, Pen. I'm sorry. We have to talk about it. I can't do it after all. No matter what I want them to save me so I can be here with you and the kids. I changed my mind."

"Don. Don't do this to Faith and Chad. Please."

"Let's talk tomorrow when Faith's not here. I still want to fight."

It broke my heart on so many levels. I'd respect his wishes, of course, but I couldn't believe he was putting himself – putting us – in this position. When it was time to leave he said, "Bye, FeeFee."

I told him I loved him.

"I love you, Pen. No matter what, I love you, too."

Chapter 60

Rubberband Woman

October 31, 1999. That night was undoubtedly the single most exasperating night of my life. I took the kids to their therapist appointment and while I was waiting my beeper went off. It was Don's oncologist with the news that the insurance company was kicking him out of the hospital. The seizures were considered stable as they'd ever be and there was nothing more that could be done for him. This was at 4:40 PM. The doctor wanted to know whether I wanted to send him to a rehab hospital. They wanted him out by 5:00 PM.

"You can't ask me to make that kind of decision in twenty minutes."

"I'm not, Penny. The insurance company is. By the way, if he's going home, he needs to sign the DNR. You'll have to force him."

"You don't know Don that well. No one can force him to do anything."

We hung up and I called Don's neurologist who said Don had broken out in a rash all over his body, the fourth reaction to the fourth anti-seizure medication.

"I've got nothing left to give him, Penny. We're out of options. Have him sign the DNR and take him home."

The rash bought me an additional twenty four hours to make a decision since it was considered life threatening, but Don was refusing medication to control it until we got to the hospital. He wanted to be awake to enjoy his kids.

Then when I was on the phone again with the first doctor, the therapist came out and said, "I know Don needs you to make decisions for him, but Chad is very bad. I need you to hang up. Don's got to wait."

I put Chad on my lap and held him while he sobbed. The whole time he was in the hospital fighting leukemia he never once cried like that. Then Faith came out crying, too. I became a rubber band, exercising the extent of my rubber-like qualities and all too ready to snap. It took everything I had to stay in my body. If I were superwoman I would have whisked the kids out of there pronto, but I was a mere mortal and a mother at that. All I could do was let my heart break right along with theirs, the seams that held it together cracking and popping like logs in a campfire.

When we finally regained some sense of equilibrium we left for the hospital. I closed the door to Don's room and in front of Faith and Chad asked,

"Do you want to come home and live with us? Sleep in a hospital bed downstairs with nurses attending to you during the day? You can have dinner with us, watch T.V. with the kids, do magic with Chad, and read with Faith?"

"Yes, that's what I want."

"Then you have to sign the DNR."

"I don't want to give up yet, Pen. I want more chemo. I want another opinion on the MRI."

"Don, there is no more treatment unless you get stronger. In your condition, you'll die from the chemo or radiation first. We're done."

"He looked at the kids, "Do you want me home?"

"Yes," Chad said. "But you have to get stronger. Mommy can't take care of you like this."

Don's doctor said he needed to make the decisions tonight. Don told us how scared he was to leave us. Faith and Chad told him what an amazing father he was.

"There's nothing that needs to be done, Don. You took care of us as best you could, you expressed all your wishes for us, and we've made your dying wishes happen. It's okay to go."

Surprisingly, Chad and Faith agreed.

"You taught me your magic secrets and I'll be a famous magician when I grow up."

"You shared a lot with me, Dad," Faith said. "It's okay. We'll be okay."

I called the doc and said as soon as his rash is cleared I'd like him sent to Linwood Convalescent Home. I guess there's a new sheriff in town, although I'd do anything to turn this badge back in. We left Don and went home to pretend to enjoy Halloween. After all this was the *living life to the fullest* part, hoping the kids would remember a few fun moments.

Of course, the next day when I called he sounded fine, perfectly normal, alert, and funny. He asked the kids how their Halloween went. We brought him candy at the hospital and found him to be mentally fine, but physically weak.

Physical therapy came. It took a man on each side and a walker to get him to walk twenty feet. They did some exercise and an assessment. Debbie, the social worker and our former babysitter, came. She said Don had zilch for short term memory, but could probably pass his dental boards right now because his long term memory was intact. He didn't remember stuff that happened ten minutes ago, but recognized her immediately. She told me if he continued to walk with assistance he could come home with a hospital bed, commode, walker, wheelchair, ambulance assistance to physical therapy daily for four hours a day (the other twenty are up to me!). If he can't walk, all bets are off and it's a nursing home for him, not as cozy, no dinners with the family, no T.V. with the kids, just an anonymous room with an anonymous caretaker.

But option one was not an option unless Don signed the DNR papers which he wouldn't because he still wanted to fight. Debbie says chemo and radiation will make him weak and kill him more quickly. He doesn't want to hear it.

When I left I bent to kiss him and he said, "Don't kiss me. It hurts my ear and head. Just kiss my hand. But I love you and tell the kids I love them very much."

I cried all the way home. It saddens me that my husband's choosing to spend the last days of his life fencing with windmills, looking for a victory where none can be had. He had no chance, yet he was still drawing sword.

And what of us? Where were his thoughts for us right now? For wouldn't it be better to die among family rather than spend your final days in the sterile environment of a nursing home?

My father-in-law said he'd made his decision. "Let's give him his wishes and wait to hear what Dr. Freid says. Send his MRI to New York and see what their opinion is. By then he may have regained strength.

Don told Debbie he wanted to void his living will, and that he wanted to fight, and to be saved at all costs.

"Penny is superwoman. She can handle it."

"You're wrong, Don," Debbie said. "Penny's tired. She can't take care of you one hundred percent of the time without nursing help. She's still got the kids to care for."

"I'm going to take her out next week to dinner and a movie. We'll have Thanksgiving as a family."

I guess it's not out of the question, but I didn't see that written on the wall.

I do have one light moment to report. My brother Mark flew in from Texas to see Don and caught him in a lucid moment. He told Don that he'd see him again in a couple weeks, but if for whatever reason he didn't, to tell God the same advice he'd given to so many down here.

"What's that?" Don asked.

"Remind him to floss."

Chapter 61

Porno Penny

November 3, 1999. What a difference a day makes. Okay, so I was still smarting from Don's decision to void his living will, but that doesn't mean I'd shut down. I was determined to grant each and every one of his last wishes if for no other reason than to avoid the guilt! But that didn't mean I couldn't still kvetch on cue.

"You know, I didn't like it when you called me superwoman. It's unfair. I can't handle your needs alone."

"I know. I'm sorry, Pen. I just meant it in a devoted way. Not selfish. To me you are super. I see how the kids cling to you, petrified. I see how you've put us all first. I'm just not ready to leave you yet. There are still things I want to share with you."

I cried, of course, but I was just as grateful for the lucidity with which he communicated as for the apology. It had been months since we'd had a heart to heart and the strain of it was weakening me. But today – aaahh, today. I sat on the bed. We held hands. I even gave him a sponge bath and zaftig that I am and not much for weightlifting or exercising of any kind really, I lifted him. Imagine that.

Lunch was great because Don was so amusing. He told me about how the nurses are always pulling on his catheter and when he objects they say, "Oh, no biggee, just the catheter."

"And where do you think it's attached?" he responds. "When I checked in I was an average guy, size-wise. By the time I check out, my penis will be dragging on the ground."

I was howling. I guess even in death size matters!

Other than the fact that Don has very little control over his body – and yes, that means he defecates in bed without warning (and then denies it), we had a wonderful, intelligent day together.

When I got home I found I'd been locked out of my AOL account. Reason given? Those nice people at AOL thought, due to the sheer volume of people I send email to, sometimes upwards of a few hundred at a pop, that I must be trafficking in porn. So they shut me down. I explained that there was really nothing even remotely sexy about brain cancer and after conferring with the managerial staff it was decided I'd be placed in the pornographic section which would allow me to send "unsolicited material" along with the other pornos. So hey, let me know if you want me to write you a dirty email. I'm sanctioned. It's legit. I'm kosher.

I see a whole new future on my horizon.

Chapter 62

Wife From Hell

I've gained weight. And it's not some change of life thing, peri-menopausal, hormones raging out of control thing. It was the sheer weight of life that had been added to my own body mass. It was a couple ounces of fear, a few of trepidation, the loads and loads that misery piled on, and not to forget the pounds that grief was about to throw at me. Add the weight of my anger, and a host of other unpleasant emotions and it was no wonder I put on another ten pounds. I should have thrown those Tootsie Rolls away, but I doubted it would make a difference. You can't throw away your emotions, and those were the true culprits here. I wondered which weighed more: fear or depression. My money was on depression. At least with fear you were offered the fight or flight option, but depression just kept you down. There must be a whole kilo of extra weight that comes along with depression. Thank God I'm not there yet.

They moved Don to a sub acute care unit close to our home and without the protracted wait that was indigenous to these moves. I asked, somewhat stunned, how it all happened and so fast. I shouldn't have been shocked at the answer.

"We're small town people around here, Penny. We know your family history. Don was a local doctor with a lot of friends. He played tennis with all the big shots in town. Of course, we'd move mountains for him.

So that was done. But now my latest predicament was that the kids didn't want Don to come home. Not unless I sold our house the second after he died.

"Daddy's too spooky," Chad said.

"I'll never go downstairs again if he dies down there," Faith said.

I believed her. She was exactly like her father. Of course, Dr. Freid needed to evaluate the MRIs first. Don would be devastated if there was nothing left to treat him with and maybe worse, I'd be stuck with two shell-shocked children. Just for today, though, I didn't need to worry about making a decision.

So I focused on Chad who was due for his monthly blood work to make sure if he was still in remission. He'd better be or I was sticking my head in the oven and since it was electric, I was probably going to get split ends. Meanwhile, I found out the day before that

Don got none of his meds all day and his seizure level was extremely high. When I called, the nurse gave me a little attitude.

"I have no idea why his needs weren't met. I just signed on."

So I called Don's neurologist who took over for me, adjusted all his drugs, and then called me back.

"Penny, you have to watch every move these places make. Don's too confused to remember on his own. So you'll need to be the Wife From Hell like you were the Mom From Hell for Chad."

Oy. This is why people take their loved ones home to die.

I just realized Don won't be home for Shabbos dinner – the Friday night dinner before the Sabbath begins at sundown – and we could all use some blessings now so I took the kids to the nursing home. While we're not a religious family, we do follow tradition and we do Shabbos dinner every week so the kids will have a warm memory of family dinners together. Don blesses both the children and me and uses this prayer in his blessing.

May the Lord bless and keep you.

May the Lord make his face to shine upon you and be gracious unto you

May the Lord lift up the light of his countenance upon you
And give you peace.
And let us all say, Amen.

I laid awake in bed that night recounting those words alongside all the things Don was not about to see: our future together; Faith's prom dress; Chad getting his driver's license. I was ready to trade back in this lousy hand, God, and make a better deal. What do I have that I can give you? What of mine will you take? Oh, that the double-meaning of that last question was lost on me.

Chapter 63

Fruit Salad

My husband was dying and he didn't even know it. The MRI review results were back. Even Dr. Freid was throwing in the towel. I didn't have the stomach to tell Don, "It's over, Babe. Time to lay down your sword. No more chemo. No more radiation. Just give into it, because you aren't getting out alive."

But I was afraid. Afraid of life without him. Afraid of more of this life with him, being as I am after all these cancer-filled years, totally zapped. I'd take another step if I could, but I was in an emotional black hole where nothing comes out, a place from which not even light escapes.

"Don't die," I wanted to say. "Please. Stay with me," and in the next breath, "Please God, take him. Take him quietly. Take him soon."

He was tearing at the remaining tenuous seams that held our family together with his inability to remember whether he just pooped or ate lunch. I tell him there's no hope.

"Damn the doctors. I want to fight. For you. For the kids...."

And he was strong, damn it, so strong. Damn his muscular body and his low-fat foods all these years. A lesser man would have folded by now. I hate your willpower, your ability to keep even Death occupied in the waiting room for far longer than He wants to be. "Shut up," I want to say. "Listen to the doctors. It's your time. There's nothing else to be done." But I'm mute. Don's will shall be done. After all, it's his death. Shouldn't he get to choose? I fight myself for control. I wonder if *shut up* counts if you never say it out loud.

And then, as if by magic, it fell into place. He remembered he has to get out of bed to use the bathroom. He could walk on his own after being told he might never walk again. His speech was coherent. His therapist asked him to name his favorite fruit.

"Richard Simmons," he replied.

The staff roared at his witty retorts. He had a new audience. I bunched the corner of my shirt in my hand, over and over, a repetitive motion that kept me from screaming, but would probably give me carpal tunnel.

Still, even the wit can't obscure the knowledge that he looked, smelled and acted differently. I thought about the things that first attracted me to him: his great character, strong will, love of life. I try to dwell on the good, but the scary pukey stuff keeps inviting itself to lunch and I'm too good a hostess to decline. And all those things I concerned myself with: what type of coffin to pick; what his headstone should say; where to bury him; Don didn't care about those things because he would be dead.

Such matters were strictly for the living.

Chapter 64

And Duke Says...

November 11, 1999. Don beeped me.

"Pen, I woke up with the Rabbi doing a blessing over me and I thought, 'Shit, I'm dead.'"

He may as well be. Duke called tonight. I had just gotten Don settled in his room so I took the call in the hall. Duke said they were surprised Don was still walking around and not in a coma. Afterward, I asked Don if he wanted to come home, that I would sleep downstairs with him. He said when he gets stronger so he can use a cane and we can sleep upstairs. Duke said not to reduce the steroids by even a milligram or he'd seize. Apparently, every minute counted now.

Before I went to bed, I squeezed the kids while they were in their bed as best as one can a sleeping child, then settled in myself. But I was restless and scared and wanted to talk to Don about what Duke had said. It was after midnight, but I called anyway.

The phone rang and rang incessantly until I couldn't stand it any longer.

"Don, pick up," I begged into the receiver. "I have things to tell you. To share with you." I cried, I cajoled, I pleaded, but the phone continued its inexorable ringing. "Don, please," I breathed. Nothing.

I called the night nurse who said, "The phone's on. If he's awake he should pick up. I called back, let it ring longer – "Please, please, please, Don, I want to tell you about the kids, the car, the house, the mail, a million little things like I always do."

Then it hit me. He's gone. He doesn't even exist anymore. All week I'd been to visit and he'd been to physical therapy or sleeping. And even though his body was there, he was gone. My future was swirling, counter-clockwise, I believe, waiting for a final tug from gravity to pull it down the drain and banish it forever.

The next morning I got dressed to the nine's and went to see my husband, but when I got to his room he wasn't there. I found him being wheeled down the hall, coming back to his room.

"Why are you playing hide and seek with me?"

He smiled as if Ed McMahon had just handed him one of those oversized checks. I told the aide I'd take him from here and in the middle of the hall hugged him so hard I heard his bones pop. I told him about my frantic midnight attempts to reach him – he'd heard the phone, but couldn't get to it – and then we went to a pizza party on the floor. I didn't tell him the latest assessment; no need to spoil our date. We were laughing, holding hands. Don was bopping to the music in his chair. A man, about seventy, burped really loudly.

"Make sure I don't do that when I reach his age, Pen."

"I promise I'll never let you embarrass yourself."

He still had such hope and I never wanted to take it from him. Afterwards, I took him back to his room and tucked him in for a nap. I told him I was taking Faith shopping for the night unless he preferred I stayed.

"No. She needs the time alone with you. Buy her nice stuff."

Faith and I went on a shopping spree to the mall, about two hours from our house. A girl's night out, just Faith and I, on a date. We decided to come home instead of sleeping in a motel. At about 1 AM I heard someone open my bedroom door. I sprung up, wide awake.

"Don?"

"No, it's me. I thought I heard someone walking around."

"Faith, you scared me. I'm not walking around. I'm sleeping."

"Mommy, you yelled out for Daddy. Daddy isn't here. He couldn't help you even if he was."

A valid point. "Give me a kiss and go back to sleep," I said. Faith shut the door and I cried myself back to sleep.

At 2:50 AM, the phone rang. It was Don.

"Hello?"

"Hi. What's up?"

"I just wanted to tell you to bring something when you come see me tomorrow."

"Okay, what?"

"You. I want you to bring you."

I started crying again then asked if he was having an okay night.

"Not really. A lot of accidents in my bed."

"That's all right. I've got plenty of extra underwear for you."

Then I told him what happened with Faith and he said, "See, Pen. You aren't ready to let me go."

"Don, come home. We'll sleep downstairs. It'll be okay. You'll see.

"Not yet. But I'm glad you didn't stay in a hotel so I could call you like this. It's like we're talking in the middle of the night in our own bed – like we used to."

Then I told him about the mall, visitors, his birthday present, talking until we grew tired.

"Penny?"

"Hmmm?"

"I'm really glad I met you. You made me happy."

"I'm glad I met you too. I love you, Don."

I wish I had that phone call on tape. I would have kept it forever.

Chapter 64

Treasure Chest

November 13, 1999. Don was really going downhill tonight. He was in full diaper mode now, needing help to be pulled up in bed – still very funny although slow to respond, his head drooping to one side, like he had a rubber neck. I half expected to see drool running from the side of his mouth. Chad went ballistic in the car going home (and Chad doesn't scream – Faith's the screamer). I didn't know what was worse: Don, or Chad's reaction to him

"There's no way he's coming home like this. My God, he's so weird. He isn't Daddy anymore. You better not bring him home."

Faith was much more understanding and compassionate. She didn't mind hanging out with him even if he didn't respond. I asked her what she thought about him coming home.

"He can come home. I just don't want him to die there. Let him come until it's almost the end and then put him back in."

"Faith, honey, it doesn't work that way."

Meanwhile, Don doesn't want to come home yet. He was working on journals for me, Faith and Chad and wanted to finish them first. He wasn't unhappy there. He loved the food, got along great with everyone, and was even goosing the nurses with that funny grabber cane they gave him. The nurses thought I should leave him where he was as long as insurance was paying because of the work intensive nature of his care. They also thought he was slipping quickly. Had I known then how tough my husband really was and how long he would continue to defy death, I would not have even considered bringing him home. There's just no way I could have handled that kind of twenty-four hour care for that kind of time.

So right now we were just hoping for a few more nuggets of gold in the form of lucidity, recognition, and stolen moments of love and laughter – the treasures of life. We would take whatever we could get.

When I put Chad to bed he said, "Daddy's going to be dead by morning, I know it."

"I don't know, Chad, but I'm glad you got to see him tonight."

"You know how you say we'll still have fun once Daddy's gone. How we'll still go on vacations and do fun things?"

"Yes."

"Well," he said, near tears, "no offense, Mom, but Daddy's the fun one. All you like to do is sit in the shade by the pool. Daddy's the one who does the archery and the boating and swimming – all that cool stuff."

I laughed. "You're old enough to know the things your father would have loved to do with you. Also, something tells me you'll make your own fun."

Then Faith came in crying. "Everywhere I look there are pictures of Daddy with us. Smiling, happy occasions. This is so sad, Mom. It just doesn't make any sense.

The next morning, I called my Mom because I knew she had gone to visit Don.

"How is he?"

"Very bad, Penny. Very bad. I left there crying. He's not making sense. I just can't stand to see him like this."

I didn't tell the kids, just packed them up and went to the nursing home. Chad ran ahead like he always did, excited to see his father, only this time he came running out of the room.

"Mom, something's wrong. Daddy's real bad."

I went running down the hall and found Don laying with the bottom half of his body on the bed and his head and torso off, legs splayed, wet underwear, arms spread and eyes wide, but snoring, dead asleep. I thought he was in a coma because I touched him and he didn't respond.

Chad was crying, Faith staring in shock. I told the kids to run and get the nurse and right then he looked up and started shaking all over, closed his eyes and went back to sleep, or whatever it was he was doing, opened his eyes about ten seconds later, turned his head to the kids and an in clear voice said:

"I - don't - want - my - kids - to - see - me - like - this - anymore. Please – have them go - away. Sorry kids."

They took off running. It was terrible. I asked Don what was up, why he was in that position, but he just kept following me with he eyes. The nurse had no idea, having just come on. I put a diaper on him, had the nurse change the sheets and crawled in bed with him. The kids came back, still scared, but Chad took his hand and Faith told him what an incredible father he was.

He looked us all up and down before he said, "You're my whole world, you three. Thank you. I love you, but I don't want you to remember me the way I was before." He squeezed Chad's hand. "Don't fight. Listen to your mother. She's amazing. I knew the first night I met her. That's why I married her."

Faith started crying and Chad hid himself in Don's curtains. I hugged him, trying to hold the moment for a bit longer. Then we all kissed him goodbye, told him we loved him and would be back early, but he'd already fallen back to sleep. Driving home I explained to them that what they witnessed was the worst thing they could have seen and if they forget that and just remember the final lucid moments where he said goodbye, that should be comfort enough. Neither one of them spoke, just cried.

I called Don's parents who had a bag packed and were ready to walk out the door if he didn't get through the night. Don's Dad had already called all the relatives to have them come and say goodbye while he could still respond. He told me he was going to meet with the funeral director in the morning to pick out a casket and that I should hire a caterer for as many people as I thought would come to eat and just send him the bill. Everyone should have such in-laws.

When Chad got up the next morning he rushed into my room and in a hurried voice asked, "Is he dead?"

"I don't know, Chad. No one's called yet."

So we got dressed and went to the nursing home and there was Don, waiting for us. I wanted him to dress because I knew he was expecting a lot of company. He gave me and the nurse a hard time and hid in the bathroom for awhile, but finally relented, allowing us to dress him and wheel him outside. Tons of relatives came by, many made him laugh, some made him cry, some stayed too long, all day long a litany of people coming to pay Don their last respects. What a great day he ended up having.

Faith kept saying, "I never thought after last night we would ever see Daddy so happy, smiling and laughing so much."

And Chad, "Like Mommy said. It's a gift."

Chapter 65

I Just Called...

It would have been my turn to sleep, but Don woke me at midnight.

"I just called to say I love you," he half-purred, half sang.

Stevie Wonder's got nothing to worry about, but it wasn't the singing that had me shaking, my heart pounding like a jack hammer from the wake up. Don was aggravated that one of the nurses kept slamming doors and although he'd asked her nicely to stop – "With all the steroids I'm on, the noise makes me jumpy" – she refused.

"Don't start with me," she told him.

Feeling somewhat helpless from my prone and vulnerable position, I told him I'd take care of it in the morning. After a few queries, I found out that what was really bothering him was all the company from earlier in the day.

"Everyone wanting to reminisce, like I was dying or something."

We talked for about twenty minutes, but afterwards I couldn't go back to sleep. He sounded too normal, too perfect, like he could go to work in the morning.

I broke out in a sweat after we hung up.

When we arrived at the hospital the next morning, the nurse greeted us with the news that Don had fallen down.

"The only way he can stay in rehab is if you have goals and he can meet them. He was originally, but he's slipping fast. I just want to prepare you for that.

Translation: Be prepared to get kicked out on your butts.

While Don went to therapy, my in-laws and I met with the funeral director in a private room and finalized all the plans: casket chosen; obituary written; directions to my house and the synagogue prepared. All we had to do was make one phone call when the time came.

My beeper went off the minute the meeting concluded. Chad's guidance counselor asked me to come get him. That his father still had enough of his faculties to be able to sing to me the night before left

Chad feeling confused. Why wasn't his father getting better? I took him to a fast food restaurant and tried to explain things – sometimes fast food helped – and then we went to see his dad.

The minute I got there, the head Administrator called me over.

"We need you to attend a meeting tomorrow at eleven. Bring anyone you want. Even Don.

"You're kicking him out, aren't you?

"Yes. I'm sorry. He's not getting better. He needs to go somewhere to die. We'll give you your options tomorrow. Either a nursing home or your own home, but you need twenty-four hour help."

"No way, Mom." Chad said. "You can't take care of him all night long. You'll collapse."

"I won't be alone. We'll have nurses and Grandma Janet, but let's wait until tomorrow to see what they tell us."

I sent Chad off to the lobby with my Mom to study for a science test and went back to Don's room to change his clothes and put him in bed for a nap. When I got there, he kissed me like I hadn't been kissed in months, I'm talking *hubba hubba.*

"What was that?" I asked – a little flustered, I might add. He was hugging me so tightly.

"It's almost over, isn't it?"

"Do you feel like it's almost over?"

"I feel like I'm going downhill. Very weak. I have no urine control and I feel unstable this morning."

"Like a weeble?"

"Except they don't fall down. I fell over and my legs were in the air. It wasn't pretty, Pen."

"I don't know. It depends on your angle, I guess."

We were both laughing and that fast, my current switched over to tears. Light switch Penny.

Don drew a long, haggard breath. "That's how I know it's almost over. Every day's a little worse. Plus people are saying goodbye to me all the time."

"Maybe it's not over. Maybe you'll live a long time."

"Wishful thinking. At least I can still think clearly."

And then, *boom.* Just like that he fell over with me holding him which didn't seem to matter one iota. We both went down.

Boom. Just like that.

Chapter 66

Smooth Talker

The next day, smooth talker that I am, I bought my husband more time. Don's Mom and I met with all three of Don's therapists along with the head nurse. They listed his new deficits and symptoms, stated how quickly he was failing – "on Friday he could walk twenty feet and three days later barely ten" – how he doesn't respond, just stares all the time, hears them but doesn't blink, doesn't react, doesn't anything. They talked about his constant bed wetting instances how he needed help with virtually every single task, yadda yadda yadda. *Who are they telling?*

I kept my cool. "I know Don was put in here to buy time, and I know he's dying, but I also know what you don't: my husband's a fighter. If you move him, he'll know that means game over. He's waiting to get stronger so he can come home. He's not given up on that. Isn't there some way he can stay, at least until he finishes the journals he's working on?"

Sure enough, one of the therapists agreed: "Mrs. Juros is correct. We can justify keeping him here and not fatigue him physically, just meet with him twenty minutes a day to work on his journals. That should buy you another week. We'll call your insurance company. Even if he only does one sentence a day, that's progress."

Thank God. They understood. We got another week.

When we left the meeting, Don's Mom said, "Wow, I've never seen you in action, Penny. You were great. You were direct, honest, smiled politely, but they knew you meant business and you took charge of the situation. I want you on my side when I go to a nursing home."

I laughed. "No way. That's why you have a daughter. I'm retiring after Don."

I made sure Don had company while we were in the meeting and for some time afterwards so his Mom and I could go pick a cemetery plot and do some "Shiva-shopping." The plot was beautiful, off the beaten path, under a shady tree. Don was going to love it. Or at least the old Don would have. He never liked being in the sun. Later, my parents reported back that when they went to see him in the afternoon he was unresponsive. I guess it really won't matter.

So what does one do for an encore after such a rousing, uplifting day? Attend a grief support meeting, of course. As I was leaving, my beeper went off. It was Don who, after having a confused and tiring day posed the question: "Hey Babe? Wanna have a date?"

"With who?" I asked.

"With me. You looked awesome today. Can you come over?"

Typical man. He's on his deathbed, literally, and a little skin can get him all hot and bothered. I have to admit I was flattered.

"We can get something to eat or do something together."

"All right, I'll be there in a bit."

What a gift. When I got there, he moved over in bed and I got in with him. We watched "Who Wants To Be a Millionaire" and played along and then watched sitcoms and had a snack together. We talked the entire time. At nine-thirty when he started to fall asleep, I tucked him in, kissed him and laid out his clothes for the next day.

"I think it was the best date I ever had with you, Don."

"Me, too. Let's do it more often."

There's one for the scrapbook.

Chapter 67

It's Only a Flesh Wound

November 18, 1999. All right, people, we've reached the lingering stage. Had I known it would last another two months I probably would have found that bridge I was talking about earlier, but thank God I didn't? I ask: where's Dr. Kevorkian when you need him?

When I got there Don's body was on the bed, but his head wasn't. I straightened him out, but he never once acknowledged me, answered my questions or even blinked. I brought him a pumpkin tart, an oatmeal raisin cookie, root beer and a toasted buttered bagel, all of which he devoured in about three minutes. And still never made a peep. I tucked him back in bed and he was asleep in about ten seconds.

So I took a tour of "the other side," the nursing home section where we all agreed to send Don, just in time for his birthday. It was like a scene from hell. The rooms were big and pleasant, sure, and Don will have a window, but the hallways! Everyone there must have been at least eighty and they were either dancing in the halls or half undressed, singing really loudly or just plain old acting looney. The nurse said Don had no reason to come out of his room – he never does now – and we can keep the door closed. I know Don won't notice, but it's tough for the kids and me to have to see this. Don's not living anymore. He's dying. And he's doing it slowly and without dignity. And it sucks.

Chad said this morning, "I can't take seeing him anymore, Mom. I forgot the fun, good Dad. All I think of is him laying there in a seizure."

I wanted the kids to have happy memories of their father, not this horror. To drive for over two hours to witness this? If they didn't want to see him, they wouldn't have to – their choice.

My brutal honesty may be too harsh for some, but if so, WARNING. What I'm about to say may offend others; even cause some to ridicule me. If so, then be it, but it must be said.

This whole death by incurable disease thing is insane, horrifying, and had completely uprooted every aspect of our existence. And while I would fight to the finish for Don's comfort and rights, and to make sure he knew how much he was loved, and though my greatest hope then was to leave him laughing when he goes, the pain and devastation of our situation, what I'd affectionately termed *my own personal holocaust*, was just too brutal, too unrelenting, like being hit repeatedly about the head and neck with a sharp object while blood drips everywhere and me trying to catch it. Circumstances had left me in a state of shock, feet cemented to the floor, shivering against the harsh light of my most certain and lonely future without a clue as to what to do next. But what I did know is this:

The sight of my husband dying was truly disgusting.

And another thing: the clean up crew was exhausted.

Chapter 68

Wifey for Lifey

November 21, 1999. Don was starting to have back, buttock and rib cage pain resulting in him being completely uncomfortable and cranky. He only responded to me, if at all. He would hide in the bathroom for three hours, staring at himself in the mirror and since he had no concept of time, he thought it was like three minutes. Whenever he wasn't hunkered down, I sang, I danced; I did whatever I could to make him laugh. When I belted out a roaring rendition of "You Are the Sunshine of My Life," he started bopping along and after a few verses said, "You still can't sing for crap, Pen. I'm not that confused."

So I deep-sixed the acapella, put some music on and did the twist. A go-go dancer I'm not, but Don was giggling and seemed to enjoy the floor show.

Half an hour after getting home, I got a call from Don's nurse. Don had fallen. They found him on the ground and when one of the nurses asked him "what are you doing down there?" he said, "kissing the carpet." They had no idea how long he'd been there.

The nurse also told me he'd been giving her major attitude exhibited by wild and fierce mood swings, a result of the tumor taking over the brain. She also relayed that Don advised that he was being moved to a room with a view (of the parking lot) for his birthday tomorrow and he was quite happy about it.

Actually, he's being moved to the nursing home section of the facility where he'll likely die, but he'll get a window bed in the switch so to him it seems like a winning situation. He doesn't know about the nursing home part, and I won't take his hope away by telling him the truth. At least he can go down fighting to the finish, dignity intact.

When I talked to him in the morning, I asked if he'd kissed any carpet lately. He had no recollection, but laughed heartily at the story. Then he asked why I never come to visit which broke my heart. He thought it had been days when really it had been hours.

"I'm on my way," I told him.

"Good. You're my wifey for lifey. I'll just take a little nap until you get here."

I tried not to laugh.

Chapter 69

Queen of Mean

November 22, 1999. Don's 41st birthday. At the hospital, I run to his room like a five-year old, eager, all dressed up, anxious to share things with him, only to find him bloated and wincing in pain. The therapist told me he was weaker than yesterday with at least three seizures ahead of him. She had asked him if he wanted to come home and he said, "No, but I'd like to try and go home for the afternoon of Thanksgiving just to eat and then come back. But I need to talk to Penny about it." Just for the record, the therapist thinks it's a bad idea.

I tried to move him out of the chair and onto the bed to ease his pain. Bad move. Like trying to relocate an elephant. He used to have some strength, could push with his hands, but today, nothing.
I almost broke my back.

While I hunched over him he whispered in my ear, "I better not come home, huh? I'm way too weak."

I didn't know what to say.

The kids think it's "way scarier" over on this side of the nursing home and I don't really know what to do with that because I do, too. Other than Don, everyone's a million years old.

The other night, Chad asked me, "Who's going to tie my ties when Daddy's gone? My brother told him there were plenty of men in the family to teach him about ties and shaving. Poor kid. He only wants his dad to teach him.

In one of Don's lucid moments, I shared with him the controversy surrounding my complete honesty on the brain tumor list (email group) and how one or two people had lashed out at me because of it. I'm not going to pretend I like watching my husband deteriorate just to spare a few feelings.

Don replied, "They don't know who their messing with. You're the Respectable Wife From Hell. The Queen Bitch. The Queen of Mean when you have to be. I have to say, I'm proud of that. It sure has helped me."

So there. Take that.

Don's orthodontist buddy visited him today, but only stayed a few minutes because Don was falling asleep. His sleep was ever increasing, up to about twenty hours a day. Tonight he started shaking and when I jumped up, he said, "its okay, Pen. It's not a seizure. It just happens now."

What kind of hell is this and who can I hold accountable for it? After all, I have a reputation to maintain.

Chapter 70

Missing In Action

November 25, 1999. We brought Don home for the day so we could have Thanksgiving together as a family. Rabbi Geller and Elaine visited him in the morning and said he was terrific so I'd hoped for the best. But by the afternoon when my sister, Judi and her husband, Marc, arrived, Don was off in La La Land and couldn't even acknowledge us. The staff helped us get him in the car and all the way home I talked about who was coming, what we were eating, and the like, but he never responded.

It took half a lifetime to get him out of the car and into the house, but once inside, we propped him up at the kitchen table we're he could talk if he wanted. Instead, after half an hour he broke out in a sweat so we put him to bed. I roused him from a deep sleep about forty-five minutes later. Maybe I should have let him sleep, but this is what he came home for, right? Dinner? He never acknowledged anyone, not even

Chad doing a new magic trick for him until we sang happy birthday to him. Don came to life at that, sang along with us, and then returned to oblivion for the remainder of the meal. His sister started to cry. She wasn't the only one.

After dinner, Chad performed magic for everyone. Even our neighbors and Laura joined us, quite a crowd, all hoping to see Don. He seemed happy although he still didn't speak as if his body was present, but his brain was missing in action.

His brother and brother-in-law took him back to the nursing home when the party broke up. We had good food, good company and a complete family for what may have been our last holiday together. If we make it to Hanukkah, it's got to be the nursing home for us. I'd only consider doing this again if Don asked.

It had been one month since Don arrived by ambulance in the sub-acute facility he now called home; one month since we got the death sentence that Don had weeks, maybe only days to live; one month that I'd been steeling myself against the inevitable; one month that I hadn't taken a full breath for fear that my lungs couldn't hold it all. If my foundation was going to crumble, I wish it would just do it already.

My heart couldn't take much more of this, watching my husband lose the use of his faculties, one by one, slowly, inexorably – and then, not. One minute he's completely out to lunch and the next, lucid, almost normal. This is a strange purgatory we're stranded in, and I'm thinking that if I'm not getting some big karmic points for this then something's wrong with the system. I have two questions: 1) my slate's got to be sparkling shiny clean after this, right? And 2) how much longer does he have?

The answer to that second one I almost can't bear to know.

Chapter 71

Happy Hour?

December 3, 1999. Well, we made it to December in this strange, cloud-covered holding pattern. For every good day Don has four bad ones, but I'm learning that doesn't mean anything.

When I arrived at the nursing home, Derek, Don's favorite therapist told him he'd given Don "what for," i.e., reprimanded him for waiting three hours before he eats, not taking control, failing to respond.

I didn't lose it as you might expect, just gently explained Don's condition. He had no idea. "He has no concept of time. He isn't trying to be mean or rude or drive the staff crazy. He just can't help it." By the time I'd finished, Derek was crying.

I touched his arm. "I cry all the time. But the doctors assure me he's in a good place when he's like that. He's happy. Not in a rush." I doubt I helped Derek much, but at least he'd be nicer to Don in the future.

When I saw Don, I told him about my conversation with Derek.

"I'm sorry for being a pain to the staff."

Those were the only words he spoke all day although his eyes lit up when I told him his parents were bringing him homemade latkes. I told him we'd be back to celebrate the first night of Hanukkah with him. He smiled and then fell asleep.

That night, the kids and I went to my parents for Hanukkah dinner. We arrived at 3:35 PM and were out of there by 4:07 PM. That's with eating dinner – delicious latkes – lighting the Menorah, singing the prayers, exchanging presents, having dessert, of course, and signing on again to check my email (of course). I can hear my brother and sister laughing now. The Goldberg's have never been known to be slow. If you asked me how it tasted, I couldn't tell you. I haven't swallowed yet.

Then we were off to see Don. When we arrived, Derek told me what a good day Don had, the best in weeks. He'd forced my husband out of bed, helped him dress all New Jersey chic (translation: a nice sweat outfit), and took him to Happy Hour. Don enjoyed himself immensely, dancing in his wheelchair, singing to the music, totally responsive. When we got to his room, I was shocked to see how great he looked, all dressed in a white warm up suit, his hair sticking up like Don King.

"Hey, I heard you went to Happy Hour. What did you do there?" I asked.

"Got happy," Don said.

I took out the Menorah I brought while Faith decorated his room for Hanukkah. We lit the candles and Don was signing the prayers, remembering every word perfectly. I asked Derek when he last had a steroid shot.

"About forty-five minutes ago."

Bingo. I knew it was drug-induced, but I didn't care. It was great to have my husband back, even if it was ever so briefly. It was like he was drunk from Happy Hour and we in turn, vicariously through him. But as usually happens in an intoxicated state, I turned my back for one minute and *uh oh.*

"Mom. Mom. Maaaaaaaaammmmmmmmmm," Faith was panicked.

There was Don, holding the plastic part of his cane above the candles, watching as it caught fire, big blue flames shooting up into the air. I could tell by the trajectory of his cane that next he was aiming for the drapes.

"Oh my GOD, Don. What are you doing?

Don, innocently: "What? What did I do? I'm just playing around."

I grabbed the cane and put out the fire just as the nurse came in, reprimanding us. "You're lucky the alarm didn't go off," she snapped. "Blow out those candles. No more fire. And no more anything," she said, turning to Don, "unless someone is with you at all times."

"What's the big deal? It was only a little fire." Don was giggling; the rest of us were in shock.

It wasn't too much longer before we said our goodbyes and, walking to the car, Faith said, "Mom, he was freaky again tonight. Like he was drunk or something. He either doesn't talk or he sets the place on fire."

"He's dangerous," Chad said. "This is why he can't come home."

I didn't want to admit it, but it was true. Hours later, I was still shaking.

Chapter 72

Festival of Lights

The next morning I went to see Don. The nurse said he hadn't spoken since the night before and he refused to feed himself. I left Chad to wheelchair races in the hall – he had a hard time being in the same room with his Dad lately – and walked in Don's room to find Faith feeding him. Sad as it was, it was a beautiful scene, one I'll always remember. As expected, Don never spoke a word to us the entire time we were there.

We went back at night – having had lit the Menorah candles at home – and although Don again never spoke a word, he took Chad's hand when we arrived. I fed him dinner I brought from home and when he was finished, I announced it was time to light the Menorah. Faith and Chad both dove for cover.

"I'll get the cane and hide it from Daddy," Faith yelled.

"I'll move the candles away from him," Chad chimed in.

We were hysterical, even Don, who confirmed my suspicion that he does hear everything, just doesn't always respond.

The next day I spoke with Don's doctor who told me he's amazed every day when the nurses give him a report and tell him Don's still hanging on. Don's cough was getting worse, and although he didn't think it was pneumonia, he wanted my assurance that I didn't want Don moved to a hospital if it turned out to be so. I took his Mom with me to see him and when we got there he was watching T.V. After feeding him a snack, we all watched "The View" together. They had a psychologist on who said if a man isn't thinking about having sex twenty-four hours a day then something's wrong. Don roared, laughing so hard I thought he was going to capsize. We were all laughing, but of course, I cried all the way home. He seems happy, but he's getting weaker, seizing almost all the time now, his arms and legs shaking constantly, as if he has Parkinson's Disease. He can't hold a drink in his hand without spilling it. He's still so sharp; his mind's so clear. He just can't get the words out. One part of me hopes he lives this way for years.

But only one part.

Chapter 73

We're Making Lovey Dovey

December 4, 1999. Don was still refusing food unless someone fed him. If I didn't know better, I'd say he was starving himself to death, but then the administrator of the home went to see him.

"What's up, Don? Why don't you eat anymore?"

Don just shrugged.

"Tell me what you'll eat and I'll make it for you."

"Chocolate sundae."

My parents arrived later to find Don chowing down on a chocolate sundae with all the fixin's. He reported to me with his eyes that he really enjoyed that meal. He's like a baby now, wearing diapers and a bib, needs to be fed, watches any show on T.V. without question, and doesn't talk because he's not there. He coughs constantly. I think he has pneumonia. I asked him if he thinks the therapy's helping.

"Depends on the day," he said tersely.

I asked, "Who put you in bed, Don?"

An honest-to-God tear fell from his eye. "I don't remember, Pen."

My own eyes watered in empathy. I'm trying to help him maintain his dignity. When any of the nurses call him Mister, I ask – nicely – that they call him doctor. They've taken to calling him "Doctor Don" and fight over who'll bathe him. At forty-one, Don's got a great body with lean, hard muscles, as opposed to what the standard fare is among the octogenarian crowd. It makes it less of a job for them and more like entertainment.

"Whatever I can do to add spice to their workday," Don said.

He's still in there.

A few days had passed, but there wasn't much to report. Don seemed to be holding steady, doing the same things day after day, but he couldn't eat on his own and would go for entire days without uttering a word. He was full of fluid which made his eyes small, almost beady looking, because his cheeks were so swollen. His eyes would tear all the time. He seemed to be hearing things in his head and was responding, but we just weren't sure who he was talking to or what they were saying. He stared all the time, as if he were watching the room so Death didn't catch him unawares. His head hung to one side of his body and he'd fall over and lie there until someone found him, yet he didn't seem phased or frustrated. He wasn't sleeping as much, and was eating less. His short term memory was shot. He couldn't walk at all now, not even two steps and had no body strength at all. Basically, he'd turned into mush. The nurses put him in a whirlpool bath. At least that he seemed to enjoy.

When the kids and I showed up for dinner he didn't answer any of our questions, but seemed to be listening to every word we were saying.

I went to get him a drink and when I came back Chad said, "Daddy stuck his hand out while I was walking by him, grabbed me and started kissing me all over my head and face and neck. He didn't say anything, just kept kissing me, so I said, 'Oh, Daddy, we're making lovey dovey.'"

I had walked in the room toward the end of the make out session. Chad was giddy and giggling, bubbling over like champagne. I said, "This was your Hanukkah present from Daddy tonight. He just gave you the greatest gift, and I'm sure you'll never forget it. I know I won't."

It was six weeks ago the doctors said Don had "about two more weeks" to live. Yet he's still here and seems quite content to be, limitations notwithstanding.

Faith said he's "chillin'." We're in yet another routine: I come in the morning to feed him breakfast and stay long enough to feed him lunch, go home to meet the kids from the bus then go back with them at night to give him dinner. It's seems less heartbreaking than last week. The peaceful moments with Don give us some comfort. But just in case, each night before we leave we all say good-bye as if it were our last.

Chapter 74

Sixteen Stops . . .

Well, I did it. I took the much deserved break everyone said I needed and invited friends from the brain tumor list to come visit for a weekend. I met them at the airport with a hand-held sign like the limo drivers do, but instead of their real names I wrote their screen names on it. These people were living my same hell and had provided me with an incredible medical and emotional support the past year. Plus they looked one hundred percent better than in their pictures. I practically jumped out of my skin when I saw them.

Our first stop was the Ocean City beach and boardwalk. Being from the Midwest with nothing to look at but acres of corn, the fact that I lived seven minutes from the beach with its awe-inspiring views shocked them in an expansive, reality bending kind of way.

"Oh my God, Penny. Do you know how beautiful this is? How often do you look at it?"

I assured them I didn't take it for granted and that I made it a point to get to the beach or boardwalk whenever possible for some quiet time. We sauntered, we strolled, we relaxed, collecting shells for their granddaughter – something I haven't done since my kids were very little – and listened for the ocean inside. (For God sakes, we were at the ocean. What did we expect to hear?) Sometimes we laughed and sometimes we cried and since it was so cold and about to rain, we went to lunch.

Second stop was to see Don, but the minute we walked through the doors they backed out.

"You write about it and we read it, but to actually see it is tough. How do you keep coming back?"

"Because it's Don and I'm excited to see him."

They waited in the lobby while I went to see Don who happened to be sound asleep.

"Out cold," the nurse said. "Couldn't even wake him for his meds."

I hugged him and kissed him and told him I wouldn't be able to come back that night because we had show tickets.

Stop three: my parent's house. Hello's to Mom, Dad, Faith, and then on to...

Stop four: Japanese food. Delicious.

Stop five involved a bit of putting on the Ritz. Penny got *faputized*, something I hadn't done for a while. Stockings, heels, the good jewelry, fur (fake), and off we went to the casinos – Showboat, the Taj. I got pretty good at losing their money.

Stop six was Resorts. We had tickets for Joe Piscopo's ninety-minute tribute to Sinatra. Of course, small town that it is, I knew the other people sitting at the table with us – hey, I know a lot of people – and it became, "My God, Penny, everywhere we go you introduce us to someone. Who don't you know?" Like I said, small town.

I had some sad moments. Don would've loved this night, the dancing, the entertainment, but overall, it was a wonderful, rejuvenating time with a few moments of peace.

Stop seven. I picked up the gang on Saturday morning, plus Chad and Faith and went to breakfast and then back to Ocean City.

Stop eight. I left them at my house while I went to see Don. I bathed him and dressed him, fed him and just when I was going to put him in the wheelchair to go to the solarium, he fell asleep. Back at home it looked like a crime scene, everyone lying around on couches, chairs and floors. Apparently, I was running them too hard. To recuperate, we watched movies and magic tricks, napping intermittently in between until...

Stop nine – dinner with Don's sister. More food, more laughter, more casinos. We picked up Laura somewhere along the way on stop ten, and an early morning stop eleven brought me back to Don.

"I see a difference in his face this morning," the nurse said. "It looks like a change has come over him."

I didn't see it. I did see he needed to get his medicine doused in applesauce in order to get it down. Yet another faculty breaking down.

Stop twelve – a tour of the South Jersey beaches and boardwalks, Longport, Margate. Stop thirteen was to pick up Faith and Chad and go to Smithville, a fun tourist trap type of place, for the afternoon. We played boat races and dune buggy races and spent hours shopping and browsing. Stop fourteen and Faith and I headed to see Don (Chad didn't want to go – too sad).

Stop fifteen was back to my parents for dinner and the final stop of the tour was the airport. The plane was delayed and I wasn't able to wait. Laundry and lunches and prepping for Chad's science test were paramount.

On Sunday night, Faith said to me, “Oh my God, Mom, we’re going to be okay again. We’re allowed to laugh and have company and have a good time. It’s just that Daddy won’t be with us.”

For eight years I’d had to make plans that revolved around wheelchairs and medicine and walkers and naps, and now here was this one weekend like a spotlight in the night sky. I wanted to cling to it, but like all light, it traveled too damn fast to keep up and that quick, it was gone. The magical escape weekend was over, leaving only the out takes and memories.

Chapter 75

I Can't Take It Anymore... So How Is He?

December 14, 1999. I went to see Don, but rather than stop at the nurse's station as I usually do to inquire how his night was, I just kept walking. Her face told it all. Something was different.

Don was sleeping so deeply, I couldn't tell if he was breathing or not. I sat on the side of the bed and held his face. It did look different. I rubbed him, talking all the while and washed the "junk" from his eyes, oozing puss from an infection. I washed his entire face and neck, straightened his bed and fixed his pillows. I related the entire weekend, told him how much we missed him, but also how the kids and I were able to laugh again. The whole time he never even stirred.

I spoke with the nurse then, and she said they had to force him to eat dinner and breakfast, that because of his deep sleep it was tough getting him to swallow.

"I think things are moving quickly now, Penny," she said. "Don is awake less and less and totally non-responsive. But it's just my opinion."

I called my parents and relayed the news, told them not to come over. "Are you sure you want to force feed him, Penny," my mom said, and in the next, "I made him chicken soup."

I wasn't sure of anything.

I was about to leave, but decided to go back into Don's room one more time. I got back in bed with him and took his face in my hands, held him and said, "Don, are you waiting for me to say it's okay to go now? Do you need my permission? Because you know you have it. We'll be fine. We'll miss you something fierce, but we'll be fine."

Then I whispered some very private things, stuff I really felt I needed to express even though he hadn't given the slightest indication that his spirit was even in the room, and told him I'd be back later with the kids.

Before I left I said, "Don, it's me, Pennybabe. I love you, Donnybabe." And guess what? He opened his eyes, looked right at me, and smiled.

Whether he knew it was me or not, I have no clue.

I went back in the afternoon – Don had woken up as soon as my parents got there – and when I came on the floor I heard him scream so I went running.

Derek, the nurse was rubbing him down, putting all kinds of creams on his body when I entered the room.

"Hang in there, Doc. I'm sorry. I know this hurts," Derek said.

The sores that were in Don's eyes he now had internally. Oozing sores and chronic diarrhea, what a pair. The tremors were taking over his body. Derek said Don was too weak for anymore whirlpool baths.

"He won't even get in the wheelchair now and he can't sit up without assistance," Derek said. "We're all broken up about it, Penny. The docs are doing what they can about the bedsores, but he sleeps almost twenty-three hours a day now. He wakes up to eat is all."

When I returned the next day, bearing a bagel, a banana muffin and a Stewart's Root beer (Don's favorites), the first thing I did when I entered his room was scream. His foot was swollen to about fifteen times the size of normal. Same with his wrist. The docs had them elevated. They couldn't do anything about his eyes or neck, all full of sores and rashes. I broke down (again – so what else is knew?), but then started rubbing his legs, his wrist, his face, wiping away his tears. He was following me with his eyes. I fed him, rubbed him, and talked to him.

"Please, Don, tell me if you're in pain. On a scale of one to ten, what is it? Shake your head. It's all I can do for you – feed you and take your pain away."

Nothing.

Then Alicia walked in, Don's favorite nurse. She looked wrecked, said she hadn't slept all night thinking about Don. She pointed to me and said, "Doc, do you know who this woman is holding you, telling you how much she loves you?"

Don pulled his head back as if for a second look and in a crystalline voice said, "Yep. That's my Pennybabe. She's my wifey for lifey. She's so sad. She's not pretty when she's sad, but she's always beautiful to me."

I threw myself on top of him crying, "Oh my God, Don, you knew it was me. Are you in pain? Just tell me that. Please."

He wouldn't speak again after that, not once.

When the nurse came back in she said, "We just talked to the doctor. He says the swelling's because of fluid buildup. He said to tell you if you stop giving him fluid he'll die quicker."

"No. If he's thirsty he should drink. If you see him dry-mouthed, put a straw to his lips. He can decide if he wants it."

Don smiled and tears ran down his cheeks. He'd heard me.

I got in bed with him and rubbed him. I told him I wouldn't see him tomorrow until dinnertime.

"I've got to take Chad to his yearly appointment at CHOP. He'll be perfect, Don, and then you can die in peace."

I rubbed his face until he fell asleep, all of twenty seconds, put his safety bars up, told him how much I loved him and then left.

I don't know how much more of this I can take.

Chapter 76

They Shoot Horses, Don't They?

December 16, 1999. First the good news and then the kvetching. Chad's exam was fabuloso. Dr. Hammer was most pleased and for the first time since 1991, Chad won't need any blood work for four whole months! I got goose bumps at that one. Stupendous news.

Now the kvetch. I couldn't be at the nursing home to give Don breakfast and so arranged for a friend to take my place. They were a no show. Completely floored me what with all the "Let me know if there's anything at all I can do to help," lines that I've been fed over and over again. Let me tell you, I was like a demon, a woman possessed when I heard the news. I mean, why offer?

So I called my hero, my dad – thank you, Daddy – and he went and fed Don breakfast. What a relief to know there are some people you can ALWAYS count on.

Of course, when I did get to the hospital, Don looked worse than ever. His one eye was swollen shut, and the other was getting there. His foot was huge. He hadn't moved his neck all day.

"It's time to start painkillers," Derek said. "Doc's hurting bad. "He winced even before I changed his diaper. I'm going to put him in the whirlpool bath even if I have to get in with him."

Derek said we could put him on either Tylenol with codeine or morphine and that he should start the next day. Due to the lateness of the hour, the pharmacy was already closed so I administered my own extra-strength Tylenol and left enough to last him until the pharmacy opened. Then I got in bed with him and I told him about Chad's visit to CHOP.

"If that's the news you've been waiting for, Don, you can go now. Chad's doing great and we'll be fine."

Don started crying and I joined him. We laid side-by-side without talking for a long time. I told him to "sleep forever," kissed him, and left in tears.

Two days later I was at the nursing home to feed Don breakfast. The list of contraband I'd brought with me that morning was extensive: one heating pad (illegal); one bottle of pain killers that Don had kept on hand for medical emergencies (way illegal); and one Victoria's Secret undergarment which I was wearing on my person (well, not illegal really, but immoral in some circles). So call the cops, right?

Don was sleeping when I got there and after about twenty minutes with the heating pad on his neck, I could see his whole face relaxed and he woke up. I sang Christmas songs while I fed him. *Oy*.

Don never said one word to me, but he laughed at all my dirty jokes, made funny faces when I asked if my singing had improved, and smiled huge when I showed him the bra I wore for my impending mammogram. I'm not sure which one of my surprises he liked best.

Faith came back with me at dinner with some cookies she made at a holiday party and fed them to Don, one by one.

"Daddy, this is the gingerbread man I made for you...take a bite. Daddy, look at the candy cane cookies. Be careful. This one has gum drops."

He followed her with his eyes, listening to every word she said, but never responded other than to chew. I wish I would have had a camera.

But the next morning was not so good. He was bloated, covered in rashes and uncomfortable looking. I wheeled him into the solarium, put headphones on and gave him a rub. He relaxed and looked so much less stressed.

"Don, I'm going to call your doctor and start a morphine patch."

Don grabbed my arm with a strength I didn't know he still had and said, "No!" Then he cried.

"Okay, okay, I won't. But I can't tell if you're in pain or not. It's not that bad yet? Is the Tylenol good enough for now?"

He shook his head yes. I wiped his tears – he seems to cry more than me now – and he fell back to sleep.

God I hate this. He's here, but not here. I know I promised thick and thin, but I roll over to emptiness in our bed each night. Empty like my heart. Will there be anything left to rebuild with, anything I can do to reconstruct what was once a vital and fulfilling existence? I was randomly displaced, like bits of a fallen icicle that lay melting in a ray of sun, powerless to pull myself to wholeness.

I went to bed early and woke up at eleven to hear Faith through the vents. I went to her room and cried with her.

"It's so horrible, Mom. Watching him shake all the time, and throw up, and seeing him in such pain, being helpless to do anything. Why does he have to die like this?

Chad heard us and yelled through the vents. "When do you think it will be, Mom?"

"Who knows, Chad," I responded.

"Well, I can't stand it anymore. I don't want to be mean, but I can't stand watching him die. Why can't he just go tonight?"

Because he isn't ready."

"Oy. Maybe we aren't either.

They shoot horses, don't they?

Chapter 77

Go To Sleep.

December 24, 1999. As soon as I walked into the nursing home I felt the doors slam shut behind me. The smell of ammonia, decay and urine, the creaking bed springs, the wads of suffering, the laughter of the lunatics, the sucky view, it all added up to death in my mind. On the way to Don's room, I scanned the halls for a knife so I could slit my wrists. Nothing.

I took a deep breath and counted to ten before I opened his door. And...he wasn't dead, just had a different look about him. I don't know what possessed me, but I laid it all out for him, telling him what I really felt, that it was time to let go.

"I won't quit on you. I'll be here until the bitter, smelly end, but if you think you're getting better, you sadly are not. And this is no way to live."

He just looked at me out of the corner of his eye, his head hanging to one side.

"I'm sorry if I took your hope away just now, but you lost this fight, Don. We'll be together again, you, me and the kids, I promise. But now you need to close your eyes and rest. I have no idea what's keeping you from doing that, but it's time."

Right then, as if in answer to my words, he seized. Now, he didn't look right when I walked in, but what are the odds? His eyes were rolling, his arms and legs going berserk. For a minute I sat there in shock. Then I put up the safety bar and went to get the nurse. I'm not going to lie to you and say I ran for the nurse, I didn't. And I hate to admit what I was hoping.

The nurse witnessed the tail end of it, and called the doctor who said to increase his seizure meds. I didn't want that. I just wanted it to be done already. I apologized to Don, in case it was something that I said that put him over the edge, but all I was really doing when I uttered those words was keeping my promise to help him die with dignity. The kids and I were tired, Don was tired, the nurses and docs were tired, our families were tired, geez, the whole world seemed tired.

"Go to sleep, Don," I said. I kissed him and walked out.

Chapter 77

O - Hi -O

Well, he didn't go to sleep that night or the next, or the next three weeks for that matter. And because the doctors told me two months ago that Don had two weeks to live I now had a dilemma: whether to take the kids on the vacation I promised them over Christmas break or stay and wait.... I tell you, I was split in two about the decision, not wanting to leave Don's side because he needed to be bathed and fed and rubbed and cooed to, and yet, not wanting to break my promise to the kids – the one where I'd promised we'd have fun again. I would have backed out, eaten the cost of the non-refundable tickets if it wasn't for Rabbi Krauss whose opinion pushed me out the door.

"Go, Penny. You have to go."

So we did and what a relief. We toured the Amish Country, spent lots of money at the marvelous malls, swam, and survived a blizzard, the likes of which I don't remember seeing in South Jersey. While away, I called home constantly. My parents assured me Don was fading, but still strong. The nurse said things looked bleak. "Enjoy your getaway while you can."

Amidst the heartache waiting for me at home and the disapproving glances of my host's relatives – caretakers aren't allowed breaks – I enjoyed myself immensely, living in the present, savoring each moment.

Chapter 78

Dramamine, anyone?

January 1, 2000. Happy Freakin' New Year. As soon as I opened my eyes this morning, I called the nursing home. The nurse said the doctor never returned the page I asked be left for him. I was going to tell him to stop the steroids, but since the doctor never called, Don had his shots this morning. The nurse said, "He looks like he did six weeks ago, sitting up in bed, eating, swallowing, taking his meds with no trouble, following everyone with his eyes."

Aaaagggghhhhh. He still didn't speak, but was no longer mottled and swollen.

"So no one stopped any drugs?" I couldn't believe this.

"No. We couldn't. But we realize this new condition is drug induced, a direct result of the steroids."

Gee, thanks. "Okay, tell Don I'll be in to see him later, and if the doctor does call, tell him I want to speak with him."

This was so typical of my husband. The little booger always did drive me crazy as anyone on his dental staff would tell you. And even if he can't do it physically, I'm sure he's mentally sticking out his tongue right now going, "nah, nah, nah, nah, nah." He's always been a fighter, never quit a single thing, so why would that change now.

I surrender. As long as he's eating and drinking then its status quo; we won't change any of his meds or do anything differently. I'll take the ride with him, however he decides to play it, and even though I'm so dizzy I think I'm going to puke.

Time to take a Dramamine.

At the nursing home, Don was alert, ate everything offered, had great coloring. I told him about our trip. I sang for him; he chuckled. I turned the T.V. on and did the Mummer's Strut to "Oh Them Golden Slippers," just as my mother walked in so we did it together, arms spread open holding an imaginary jacket, elbows bent, them pump up and down to the beat, da da da da da da da da da da da. You can ask my brother or sister for the words. I'm not good with details. Now, back three steps, left three steps, right three steps, forward three steps, all the while holding your jacket open (this giant beaded thing), and bobbing your head up and down. It's a Philadelphia tradition like soft pretzels and cheese steaks and booing our sports teams when they play poorly. Don was smiling and dancing in his bed. Not the best New Year's Day I've ever spent, but not the worst either. The Mummers need me. I could go on tour with them, teach the rest of the world what they're missing.

Chapter 79

Caregiver Careers

My mother told me if my husband dies, don't worry, you can get another husband. She was joking, of course, but it started me thinking about what I was going to do for money. Social Security paid until the kids were eighteen, about $25,000/year, but if I work and make over $9,000, every $2 earned will result in a $1 deduction from Social Security. I'm not formally educated, having only attended one year of college, and every time I tried to go back to work, someone in my family got cancer so my resume reads on the light side. On the other hand, I've been well-groomed for a career in health care. Too bad that after this, I probably won't have the stomach for it any longer.

January 5, 2000. Don growls all the time now. Growls and sweats. Growls and tremors. Growls and eats. I'm constantly wiping him off, but he never runs out of the stuff. It wouldn't be so bad, but for the smell. Today I sang, "You Are The Sunshine of My Life" while feeding him mash potatoes. He growled along with me, stopping only to swallow.

A friend of mine from the brain tumor list sent a package for Don. Inside there were at least fifty action figures and toys that spin and make noises and light up. Buzz Light Year, Woody, Spider Man, even a spinning Mr. Potato Head. It was like hitting the jackpot at Toys R Us. I'm not sure who was going to be more excited: Faith and Chad, or Don.

When I said goodbye today, Don gripped me so tightly, I couldn't break free. It took the help of a nurse to pry him loose. I had an indentation on my hand that looked like it would never go away, but unfortunately did. Don's doctor said he had at the most four weeks, but it could also be as little as four hours. How do I respond to that?

January 10, 2000. I dreamed I saw my Aunt Irene who died just before Don collapsed a year ago. In my dream she had come looking for him. The dead seeking the dying. I find a strange comfort in it.

We went to my niece Hannah's birthday party yesterday, the first family function without Don. The Great "Chadakazam" performed – his usual stellar self – and had requests to do two more kids' birthday parties. Chad was overwhelmed with performances, a way of diverting him from the horror of his dad's deterioration. After each one he couldn't wait to share with his father the tricks he performed and the audience reaction. Only thing is Don didn't react to his sharing which broke Chad's heart.

January 11, 2000. Alicia, Don's favorite therapist stopped by when I went to feed Don dinner. He'd been tremoring and sweating mercilessly during breakfast, but had calmed down. He was sporting a big bandage on his ear; they had cut him shaving, a tough job with all the shaking. He was swollen still, but hungry, his grip still strong. Alicia remarked that I was here for every meal and wondered if I'd moved in. I told her I just liked the food.

"Every time I walk by you're either singing or dancing for him."

"Hey, you should be here when I do the strip tease for him."

Don smiled. I told him I'd be back later with my strapless bra and crotch-less panties and that I'd do a lap dance. Now I need to make an emergency run to Victoria's Secrets because crotch-less panties are just something I don't usually have hanging around.

Chapter 80

TKO

January 11, 2000. How long can a spirit linger? How much punishment can a body take? When I got to the nursing home, Derek, and two of the other nurses were standing around Don, discussing whether or not to put him in the whirlpool. Derek wanted to ease his pain, but the nurses were skeptical, the reason being Don had so many blood clots in his legs that they were purple from groin to toes, dark red spots everywhere, his very life blood bursting in a fireworks display of blacks, grays and blues. Ultimately, Don's doctor was consulted. The result: Don was confined to bed; it was too dangerous to move him. What is the velocity of a traveling blood clot working its way from leg to lung and is the blood clot even traveling? I wonder if the excruciating pain of being confined to bed with blood clots and bed sores was the better of the two evils.

As the doctor examined him, Don refused to look at his own legs, turning his head away as if these bruised and bloodied appendages had nothing to do with him. My once virile husband must have been wondering about then, how the hell he'd ended up in this position.

Later that night, Derek and Don watched a movie on Mohammed Ali together. Every time a commercial came on during the preceding week, Don had perked up. He'd always been a boxing fan and despite the loss of so many bodily functions, he was still in there, although a TKO was imminent.

Don's doctor ordered him a VCR and tons of Don's favorite videos. I brought in the bar mitzvah tape, and the video of our wedding. I'd thought we'd be doing these forty years from now, but I guess we have to squeeze it in where we can.

The Rabbi, Geller and Krauss, both came in to see Don, telling jokes, kibbitzing, putting on a real floor show. Then they recited the Shema.

"Sh'ma Yis'rael Adonai Elohaynu Adonai Echad."

Here O Israel the Lord Our God the Lord Is One.

Rabbi Krauss asked Don if he could say it with them. Don spoke a single word: *Shema.* He hadn't spoken in six weeks, but managed to say probably the most important word in the Hebrew language. Don and I held hands the entire time. It was the most fun we'd had in weeks.

January 13, 2000. The past few days have been sheer hell, a real nightmare: better; worse; better; worse, but now it's really worse.

When I got there to give Don breakfast, five people were standing around his bed. The head nurse, Geri, said there'd been a drastic change in Don as of last night. The nurse changing his diaper said she was going to keep it loose because of the blood clots.

"Make it super tight. Cut off circulation. Tie something around him. I can't stand this anymore," I screamed. "This is no way to die."

Geri put her arm around me and said, "I'm sorry. You know we can't do that."

"Just give him something."

"We can't."

I fell to my knees and began to cry. How well I knew that. Geri patted my shoulder and helped me to my feet.

"Can I stay here tonight?"

"That's up to you," Geri said, "but I think it's going to be that soon." She squeezed my hand. "Have you given Don permission to go?"

"A million times."

"Did you tell him you'd be okay?"

"Yes. Over and over." Then I turned to Don: "I hope you win all your tennis matches in heaven and enjoy all your Star Trek reruns. I love you. I'm your wifey for lifey."

Then I left.

Alicia and Geri walked me out to my car, offered to call me a cab.

"I'm alright. I've got to feed the kids, do the homework thing. You know, normal stuff. I won't drive off any bridges."

Alicia gave me a hug.

"I guess I need to decide if I'm coming back later. I'm not sure if I want to witness Don take his final breath."

I had trouble breathing the whole way home.

Chapter 81

The Power of Love

We're all alone in this world. We're born alone, die alone, even in a crowded elevator we're alone. I'd been trying to console myself with this thought as I watched my husband die. But it was little consolation. Don and I picked each other out of a crowded room, two teenagers taking their first tentative steps in life. His mother had chastised him, wanted him to play the field some more, after all, "You're still so young, you have the rest of your life ahead of you."

His reply: "Mom, why would I want hamburger when I already have steak?"

That was the thing about Don. He was always so sure of me, of us, always put me up on a pedestal, whether I deserved to be there or not. And now he was slipping away. The crowd was dispersing and I was left, standing alone in a huge room, unsure of which exit to take. All I'd ever known was what I was doing then, or some variation of it. And soon, ladies and gentlemen, the curtain was going to fall and it would be a wrap. If the bottom fell out, that would be one thing, but it had been falling for so long with no sign of relenting that it was all I really knew anymore – free falling.

That night, I went to feed Don dinner and his head was hanging and he was propped up in a weird way. The doctor said it was over, no hope for any quality of life. Don could hear but he couldn't see us anymore. I don't know how they knew this. He shook constantly and rattled in his throat from fluid build up. He rarely woke up, and they gave him his seizure meds while asleep. They poured it down his throat. They had stopped even his liquids because he choked on everything. I stopped the steroids after consulting with Don's dad. Don would not want to linger this way.

I didn't sing to him once all night, couldn't think of one song I wanted to sing except for a rap song, and his rattle wouldn't cooperate. I held his hand all night, rubbed his head. I spoke a bit, but basically, I was talked out, tapped out, worn out. Stick a fork in me, baby.

January 15, 2000. When I got to the hospital in the afternoon, I tried to feed Don Jello and broth, but he kept choking so I gave up. I had the nurse help me move him over in bed and I crawled in with him. I slept great, better than I had all week, lying on his chest as if I still could, as if nothing in the world were wrong. I got up early and watched him sleep. Somewhere in that bloated and bruised mound of flesh, I spotted my husband, the man I loved.

The nurse came in and tried to give him liquid meds, but he choked on them so she stopped.

"If you want to be here for the end, I wouldn't leave him anymore," she said.

"You've been saying that all week," I shot back. I climbed back in bed with Don and whispered, "Is it okay if I go eat something and come back after I get the kids ready for bed?"

He squeezed my hand, but never opened his eyes.

"I'll be back later then. I'll stay the night. My mom's going to stay with the kids."

Don squeezed my hand again. He was okay with it.

It was that night that Rabbi Krauss came to say a healing prayer over him. I was going to go to the beach and look at the view. My usual habit was to climb to the top of the lifeguard stand and cry and scream and ask the air, or God, or anyone who could hear me why this was happening to me and my family. It had started to snow that evening so instead of taking the beach walk, I was on the other side of the nursing home when I heard screaming,

"Pennnnnnyyyyyyy."

I looked at the nurse and said, "oh that little bugger. He waited for me to leave the room to die." I went running down the hall and there he was, sitting up, looking absolutely gorgeous as ever. I immediately thought, *oh my God, another miracle.* His eyes were open and he smiled real big when he saw me, the first time he'd opened his eyes in days.

The Rabbi said, "Don, do you know who this woman is?" and without skipping a beat, Don replied, "That's Pennybabe. My wifey for lifey." He took my hand and I started crying. He brushed away one of my tears.

Then the Rabbi said to Don, "We're here to say the healing prayer for you. Do you remember your Hebrew name?"

Don looked at me and replied, "Chaim David."

I touched Don's face and said, "Don, Chaim David means Chad David. You're Hebrew name is Divre Levy, you're Donald Lewis."

Don looked first at me and then the Rabbi, squeezed my hand and said, "Pray for Chad. There's no more hope for me." He closed his eyes and never opened them again. Those were the last words spoken in his life.

This morning, a fuse blew and exactly one half of my house was dark, an apt metaphor for my life. Today, before I fell asleep on Don's chest, I talked and he listened or at least I think he listened. I talked about the things I'd planned on doing, the trips we'd take, the places we'd go, the people we'd meet, me and the kids, without him in our lives, "but always in our hearts," I'd said.

Will there be any space left in there, some place without bruises, some unbattered and safe place to store our memories? Does such a place still even exist in my heart?

Chapter 82

Death Watch

January 16, 2000. *Am I holding you here, Don? Is my love for you somehow tethering you to this bed, this body? If so, you can go now. There's nothing left for you.* He was still here, my husband, in a deep, peaceful sleep, thanks to Morphine.Everyone was on alert, the Rabbis, the funeral home, the relatives who were arriving in droves. No chance of being lonely, I'll say that, but it was a little tough keeping up. Since August, Don had been trying to get his wedding ring off, but couldn't. Today, my brother, armed with a truckload of Vaseline and sheer willpower slipped it off with a soft *pop*. It's my plan to pass it on to either Faith or Chad.The nursing home administrator came in today even though it was Don's day off. He said he'd dreamed about Don and needed to see him for himself, despite the hour commute it took to do so. He said our family had touched his staff so deeply that thirty-four people asked off of work for Don's funeral.

Between them, the dental community, Don's patients and our family and friends, Rabbi Krauss was planning for two hundred at the grave, another five hundred at the synagogue. *Oy.*

The kids came to see Don today. They'd not been here in a week, but given his peaceful demeanor and a bit of makeup one of the nurses applied, I thought it would be okay. Chad looked, but didn't touch. Faith kissed him goodbye. My mom stayed with him, so I could go home and take a nap. I planned on going back for the night.

When I got back, the nurse came in. She said she had to change Don more than three times now that the meds were helping him release all his fluids. All the puffiness, a constant reminder of his suspended state of living, was draining out of him along with the last precious bits of life force he still clung to. His loud, haggard breath was, like General Custer on his lone hill, also taking its last stand.

He looked a bit jaundiced in a newborn sort of way, but given how long it had been since his face had been kissed by an actual sun ray, it made total sense. We spent the night together in Don's hospital bed, wrapped in each other's arms. Other than the occasional squeeze from him, there wasn't much response. My Dad arrived the next morning so I got up, had breakfast and crawled back in bed with Don, snuggling in as close as I could get.

It was 9:22 AM. I rubbed noses with him and said, "Do you wanna hear a joke?" No response, so I told it anyway.

Still no response.

"Oh, come on, Don, that was totally your sense of humor."

He made a slight, guttural noise.

"You *are* laughing. I knew you would like that one"

About five seconds later, I realized it was his last breath. In five minutes he was cold, in ten gray, in half an hour, he was like stone to the touch. I didn't move. I just laid with Don for about 20 minutes and only I knew he was gone. It was the most peaceful time I spent with Don in a very long time.

I left him laughing in the end, though. I kept my promise after all. And I finally felt at peace and grateful. What better way to die but laughing in the arms of the woman you'd loved since you were fifteen years old?

Chapter 83

The Impossible Dream

From about six minutes after Don died until weeks later, life became strange, alien, reaching levels of chaos even I had not even imagined possible. Not one thing I'd done in the last forty odd years prepared me for this next step: life as a widow.

We held Don's funeral two days later on a sunny, freezing afternoon – if it was twenty-five degrees at the beach; imagine the world elsewhere – among throngs of friends and family, some of which we hadn't seen in decades. In Don's casket we placed a magic wand, a deck of cards, one of the first rockets Chad and Don made together, a Star Trek action figure, a tennis ball, a toothbrush and a picture of the four of us at Chad's Bar Mitzvah. About four hundred people attended Don's memorial service, so many that the cops showed up to direct traffic. The eulogies were funny, uplifting and heartfelt. I played "Just You and Me" by Chicago, Don's dying wish. It was the first song we ever danced to and, of course, I cried. I also played "To Dream the Impossible Dream" as Don requested.

I gave an eight-page speech and did not cry, although I would have liked to, while many in the audience did. The next day I heard Don's watch go off – a signal that he needed his meds – and I was immediately reduced to tears. My caretaker career had reached an abrupt end and me still wearing the "Team Juros" uniform. I filled my time walking around in tight circles. I'd have given anything for my husband to walk in the door, laugh and say, "How'd my audition go, Babe? Did I get the part of the leading man?"

Chapter 84

Funeral For a Friend

January 21, 2000. He was a creature of habit, my husband. He was brutally honest. He believed in the power of family. He wore his heart on his sleeve. He was quiet with a marvelous sense of humor. Even though he was a brilliant, talented dentist with a successful busy practice, he made sure he was home for dinner every night. He loved to build things with his hands: rockets, model airplanes, cars, whatever. He loved tennis and magic. He loved his children and me. He restored a 1952 Plymouth Cranbrook and showed it at antique car shows. Once he built a wood front end for one of his old cars and the motor vehicle inspector asked if it came with a termite certificate. It passed inspection. Even faced with death, he set goals for himself, like making a journal for each of us, me and the kids. He had big dreams for us; me, Faith and Chad, and hopefully we'll make them come true. A year ago Don had hair. A year ago he worked in a profession he loved. A year ago, patients, family and friends looked forward to seeing him. A year ago Don could run, pick up his children, dance, return a backhand straight down the line, and hold me in his arms. A year ago our lives were so full; we didn't have enough baskets and drawers for all our good fortune.

Ever since the day we got Don's diagnosis there was been a franticness associated with our lives like jumping from a plane and realizing your ripcord's been severed and your emergency cord right along with it. In such circumstances, the ground closes in fast; there isn't time to even watch your life flash before your eyes. You can either tense up, or just relax and assume the position; the outcome will be the same. The ground rises to meet you, to kiss your face, and open its cold, unforgiving arms, the ultimate release as your grieving heart splatters, a million writhing bits of hope, flipping around like fish on a hot sidewalk, struggling to find their way to open water.

PART THREE
Chapter 85

What's Left of Me Now

After Don's funeral, a massive affair, people everywhere like bees swarming the hive (proof that I'm not the only one who thought Don a honey of a human being), I entered a state of temporary paralysis but truth be told, I was spent.

The week following the Shiva, after so many people had paraded through our house all week, offering comfort and sympathy (and let's not forget all that delicious food), I collapsed, took to my bed, didn't get up for anything other than those ADLs (activities of daily living) necessary for our survival. Another one of Don's dying wishes was for me to find a nice guy and get married. Was he kidding? My husband was a tough act to follow. While Don was still alive and dying, our friend's marriage had started to crack. She said she envied our marriage, mine and Don's, pain notwithstanding, because it was solid as bedrock. And she was right. And for me to have what Don and I had with someone else, to hit the jackpot twice in one lifetime, well, was that even possible? Would some consider me double-dipping when so many others didn't even get it the first time around. The very thought kept me glued to my bed on a daily basis.

That and Grief. It was everywhere I looked and just when I thought I had stuffed it down far enough to put a toe on the carpet, it would jump out from under the bed, yank my ankle and send me sprawling across the floor, landing with a splat. I found Grief in the closet amidst all Don's clothes with their lingering smell of his cologne. I found Grief in the den every time I heard the theme music to Star Trek. Grief stood next to me at the stove when I fried Latkes. I just couldn't shake the little bugger. Then again, why should I? Grief had a right to be there, too, I suppose.

What's left of me was shredded and incoherent. I was adrift in a tsunami of rage and fear and sadness and the undertow was fierce. On occasion there'd be reason to lift my head and see the sun over the breaking waves, and on such occasions I'd laugh, only to inhale lungs full of water, the weight of which worked against me like an anchor, pulling me to the bottom of my emotional sea about the same time the trip ended. Trips like that helped with the immediate pain, like taking Tylenol with Codeine, but when the medication wore off, the pain became more acute in contrast. One minute I'd be light-headed and giddy and pain-free, the next grumpy and hostile and doubled over. The months passed in a blur. Life really is a state of mind.

Rabbi Krauss said something soon after Don's death that I've chewed on for years.

"Penny, when you look up in the sky on a cloudy night, you can't see any stars, but you know they're there. The same goes with Don. You may not be able to see him, but you know he's there."

Okay. I guess. But if he's so close, why does my throat threaten to close every time an image of him flits across my mind's eye. His little red car sat in the driveway for months until I finally sold it. For years after, I'd pull up to the house expecting to see it there. *Don's home.* Not a question, a fact of life.

But facts change their points of view, to paraphrase a famous musician. Entire history books are dedicated to facts, but they're not as static as readers and writers suppose. They're fluid and fungible and in need of air and sunlight just like everything else. And so the fact – a word I'll use as a point of reference and not necessarily as an indisputable, undeniable, frozen-in-time kind of truth – the fact is, if the future's always changing, doesn't it stand to reason that so is the past? One day Don was alive. The next day he was dead. Depending where on the time line you were standing, this event could represent a change in your past or future. You see, I've had too much time to think about things like, "If I traveled back in time at the speed of light and picked up my very much alive and healthy husband, and if we kept going at the same speed, could we outrun Death? Nothing travels faster than the speed of light? It makes sense, right?

I had four quilts made out of Don's favorite clothes. If I can't hold him, at least I can hold a part of something that held him. I presented the quilts to Faith, Chad and later my two nephews. Forever they can wrap and comfort themselves in Don.

I've found smell to be the most resolute of all the senses. It never lets you forget a memory. I discovered this little fact while on my hands and knees, routing through a pile of Don's shirts.

Those first days were definitely the hardest. We bumped through the months, Faith, Chad and I, absorbed in our own private bubbles of pain. We cried ourselves to sleep at night, and sniffled a bit sometimes in the mornings, too. That first week after Don died we had a heck of a snow storm. A father and two kids went sledding by our house. I remember we were all outside and we just stared after them as they passed, none of us saying a word. After, we went our separate ways and never mentioned it again. Chad and Don had won the local snowman building contest for the prior three years running. The year Don died, Chad didn't even enter. Those moments, they threatened daily to shift my tectonic plates, to pull me into the gaping hole that opened in my heart when Don died.

About two years after Don died, his sister decided she wanted a baby named for her brother. Since Judi and Marc could not have any more children of their own they adopted a baby from Belarus. Jared Devon was brought into our family specifically to be Don's namesake.

About four years after that Don's only brother, Michael, and his wife, Elisa had a baby boy the day after the anniversary of Don's death. They named the baby David in honor of Don.

Don lives on in so many ways. We speak of him in the present still, and no one makes a move without considering if Don would be proud. As his children grow and mature, taking on the mantle of adulthood, living their lives that in ways that I know would make him proud, I know he's always watching, beaming love to them from his alternate universe.

Chapter 86

Say the Magic Word, Chadakazaam

On January 5 2003 – three years after Don died. I was sleeping. At 2 AM, Chad came into my room and said "Mom, something's wrong." Immediately I grabbed the side of the bed for stability and strength, afraid of what was coming next.

"Mom, I can't close my eyes. I'm scared."

Now if Faith came to me and said that I'd admittedly give her two Tylenol and send her back to bed, after all she's my normal kid. But not Chad. If he so much as blinks funny I'm petrified. Of course the first thing that came to my mind was that Chad had a brain tumor. Did all that radiation cause a secondary cancer? Was all the fear that Don and I had about him having so much radiation about to come true? I knew it. *This is how it will end; Chad will end up dying just as his father did.*

I put Chad in my bed and went to the computer and wrote an email to his primary oncologist knowing that she wakes very early in the morning and might check it. At 2:02 AM, I wrote, "Jill, something's wrong, Chad just came to my room and said he can't close his eyes. Does he have a brain tumor? Is he going to die?"

Surprisingly at 2:04 AM, I received an email back from Jill. *When do these doctor's sleep?*

Jill wrote "Penny, isolated eye pain is not a sign of relapse; however, knowing Chad, something's wrong. He never complains, ever, unless it's something huge. You've done it before kiddo, you'll do it again. Get in bed with Chad, hold him close, make plans for his future and meet me at 6 AM, for an emergency MRI and CAT scan so we can get to the bottom of this."

Now I was petrified, shaking all over, because it hit me that this time I was alone. I no longer had Don, haven't had him for years. Plus my parents were in Florida for the winter. I laid in bed holding Chad's hand asking him once we get through this next hurdle where would he like to go to celebrate being well for the third time. He said he'd like to go on a cruise. So a cruise was what we planned; we focused on it for the next couple hours. Finally at 3:30 AM, I couldn't take it anymore. I got him and I dressed, packed a bag, kissed Faith on the cheek and once again disappeared into the night. At 5:20 AM, we were at the hospital waiting for Chad's doctors. At 6 AM, they took him away from me, as they have done so many times before, only this time I had no one's shoulder to cry on, no one to hold me, no one to pray with.

Once they wheeled Chad out of my sight, I called my parents in Florida. 6:05 AM. Just like the old days. When my mother answered the phone, she knew something wasn't right. She took the 7:30 AM, flight from Florida to Atlantic City and actually beat us home from the hospital. We didn't even know what was wrong yet, but how could it be good? At about 7:00 AM, Chad and I were sitting in the waiting area when a team of white coats got off the elevator. I grabbed Chad's hand and he said "holy shit Mom, this isn't going to be pretty."

"Chad, we lived here for seventeen months; we know everyone. Who are these people heading our way and why?"

"Whatever it is I'll fight it again, but let's hope for some more magic."

Meanwhile Faith was calling my cell phone because she was about to leave for school and wanted to know what was going on. I had to make these new doctors, these unknown faces wait while I took her call explaining that I have no idea but am about to find out and whatever it was, Chad was ready for another fight.

I wondered if I was.

One of the doctor's approached me and said,

"Mrs. Juros, I'm Dr. Tell, Chad's neurosurgeon. I thought to myself "Chad has a neurosurgeon?, huh." We've looked at Chad's films and we have good news and bad."

"No, no, no," I said. "You don't know me. I only deal with good news."

"You know us here at CHOP. We only deal with the truth."

Quietly, and clinging to my son's hand I said, "Please tell me the good news first so I have something to hold onto."

"It doesn't appear to be a cancer relapse."

I started to cry and exhaled for the first time since 2 AM. Well, since it isn't cancer it can be fixed, right?, whatever it is will go away and we'll go back to our normal life?. Dr. Tell went onto say "However, Chad has suffered a setback. A strange reaction to the umpteen years of chemotherapy. He's bleeding from the brain and we have no drugs to stop it."

Chad had complained this week about weak arms (*it's a flu*), then weak legs (*it's a flu*), then vomiting (*it's a flu*), but now the tests proved that Chad has a cavernous hemogioma an overgrowth of capillaries. Some people get these reddish, purplish marks on their arms or legs or even their face if they're unlucky. Chad had it on his brain – a birthmark on his brain.

"In addition to that," leave it to Chad to have not one situation but two, "Chad has a veinus angioma."

"Huh?"

"The bleed is touching a vein which means that when we open him up to perform his brain surgery, and we must or he will bleed to death, we have to nik his vein in order to stop the bleed," Dr. Tell said. "Problematically it's deep inside the brain which means Chad could be left with deficits, physical, neurological, you name it."

My son. He was one week away from being considered cured.

Chad looked the neurosurgeon in the eye, put his hand to his head and said "Please don't take the magic away from me, it's all I have left of my father."

"Chad, I don't want to take from you, I want to give to you," doctor Tell said, "but you're bleeding from the brain and the bleed must be stopped or you'll bleed to death." The doctor sighed. "Because it's hitting a vein, you'll most likely have paralysis or a stroke. At the very best we can hope you will just have severe weakness, and with physical therapy you might be able to perform some of your magic again.

Probably not the intricate minutely detailed tasks but something."

Chad was devastated. They decided on performing additional tests.

After a completely nauseating week or two of tests, tests and more tests to confirm what it was and tests to figure out how to deal with it, the docs decided that sometimes, in very rare instances (which was Chad, rare and an exception, we learned that already), pediatric cavernoma hemogiomas stop on their own. If Chad could handle the pressure and pain, then the doctor would be willing to wait a bit.

"Can I please go to North Carolina?" Chad asked. "I was just hired to perform for Richard Petty of the NASCAR world for his Victory Junction Camp. It's a camp for children with life-threatening diseases. Can I please at least perform magic there first and deal with this when I get back.

Dr. Tell replied that Chad should live life to the fullest, do whatever he needs to do to get through his pain but he had to agree to come back every week for a CAT scan to see if it had grown or perhaps stopped.

"Chad," Dr. Tell said. "I lost my father at age eleven, too and I didn't have cancer twice. Can you do me a favor? Since you're going to be at the hospital once a week, would you give me some private magic lessons. I'm actually pretty good with my hands." He laughed. After all, I am a brain surgeon. And I'm impressed with your talent and would love to learn from you." Well, that was the nicest gift he could have given my son. Whether he was really impressed by Chad's magical abilities, or just trying to help the kid out, I didn't know. But magic lesson ensued, and along with it, a beautiful friendship. Each week Chad would have his CAT scan and each week Dr. Tell would stop in for a few minutes of private lessons. They talked about everything under the sun during that private time, sharing their memories of their fathers and things about their families. And yes Chad did perform for Richard Petty and the NASCAR drivers. It was an amazing, magical experience. All this while bleeding from the brain.

The bleeding continued until May.

Chapter 87

Hora Hora Hora

In May, Faith, Chad and I were invited to Marc Fell's daughter's bat mitzvah. It was a very chic, black-tie evening affair. I had lost so much weight from worrying those past few months that I was able to wear a very sexy black gown. Faith and Chad looked awesome and we all pretended not to be worried about life and attempted to have a great time. We danced the Hora, the traditional Jewish dance where you go around in a circle, holding hands, one foot behind the other, around and around. I had Faith on my left and Chad on my right. We were smiling, laughing, singing, when Chad said "Mom, this can't possibly be good for my brain." But, it wasn't what he was saying, it was how he was saying it. Chad was slurring his words and while its easy to look clumsy while doing the Hora, it was obvious he was having trouble keeping his balance.

Oh my God, Chad is having a stroke.

I practically threw Faith at Marc asking him to be sure to get Faith home safely and steered Chad out to the car, racing to the hospital once again. Now that we were in the age of cell phones I called the hospital as I was driving. The doctors told me to keep Chad awake, keep shaking him, do not let him fall asleep. I rushed him into emergency room and they whisked him away and gave him anti seizure medicines.

Somehow we made it through the evening and in the morning they were putting the mapping on his brain to prep him for the stereotactic brain surgery when Chad said "Stop, I feel better. If you're going to take the magic away from me, please, can I perform one more time for the patients in the hospital since I lived here for so long."

Dr. Tell agreed to hold off for a few minutes and grant Chad his wish.

"We'll even tape it so we can pipe it into all the patients' rooms for years."

I ran to the car and gathered Chad's magic outfit and props, and with the leads on his head, prepared for surgery, he performed his magic show. After twenty-two minutes, Dr. Tell gave me the cut sign. Chad's speech was slurring again. It was time.

They put him on the gurney and once again Chad begged Dr. Tell, "Please don't take the magic away from me."

Dr. Tell looked at me and then at Chad and said "Say the magic word, Chadakazam," and with that they whisked him away through the double doors.

I wanted to collapse. I was scared out of my mind. Directly across the hall my world awaited me, my parents and in-laws and siblings had all arrived that quickly. They were in the family waiting room and I didn't want to go in there to speak with anyone. I wanted only to speak to one person and that one couldn't speak – Don. So instead I took a walk. My parents brought me a change of clothes so I changed from my gown to jeans. Then I went for a walk around the University of Pennsylvania campus until I'd run worry down to an idle. Only then was I able to join my family.

After seven hours of surgery, Dr. Tell emerged. He walked up to me and said "I got it."

"Did he live?"

"Yes, he lived," Dr. Tell said, "and I got it. He appears to be okay, but leave it to Chad. Not only did he have one bleed, but two. We didn't see the other one until we were inside. I had to nik his vein touching the brain twice. Most likely there'll be damage. We'll know more once he comes out of recovery."

Two hours later they moved Chad to a regular room. He was so beat up. His face was all distorted.

Dr. Tell leaned over his bed and said, "Chad, wiggle your fingers and toes."

Chad shook his head no.

"Chad, wiggle your fingers and toes. I have to see the damage I created," Dr. Tell said very sternly.

Chad shook his head no. A tear dropped from his eyes. He reached for the bedside table feeling for his deck of cards. I handed them over, and Chad proceeded to do a perfect Pharoah shuffle. A Pharaoh shuffle is one of the hardest shuffles in the magic world. It's where every single card goes between another, perfectly, quickly, efficiently, without error. It took Chad months to perfect. And here, two hours after surgery, he'd done it.

I looked over to see Dr. Tell crying. I panicked, tears running down my face. Something was really wrong if the doctor was crying. Dr. Tell looked at me and said "He appears to be perfect. Perhaps our magic boy waved his magic wand, but he seems to have no deficits."

I almost fell to the ground.

"Don't get too excited," Dr. Tell said. "I must caution you that in the next two weeks his brain will swell and there's a high possibility that he'll have a stroke."

I didn't want to hear it. For now Chad was perfect and I was the happiest woman in the world.

Chapter 88

The Magic Touch

Chad was sleeping so I did what I always did when I had a few moments – I ran to my computer to give my immediate world the good news, Chad's *magic touch.* Once again, he'd defied all the odds and came out the other side, apparently with no deficits.

I turned on my computer and there, waiting for Chad, were seven emails from seven famous magicians. Seven of the biggest names in the business wrote Chad emails, sending their regards and saying that a little birdie had told them about his emergency brain surgery, that they wanted him to heal and then get out there, to Las Vegas, that they wanted to meet him and work with him. I ran to Chad's bed.

"Chad. Wake up. Wake up. You're not going to believe the emails you received," but he was sound asleep doing exactly as ordered, healing. Once he did wake up, he couldn't even imagine who told the Vegas magicians about his surgery, and how incredible generous they were to invite him to come out for a visit.

"Mom, this could be my big break. I'm not going to let this opportunity pass me by. I'm going to practice even more than I already do," which was like, impossible, since he already did practice 24/7.

The goal of getting to Las Vegas became Chad's vision back to health. He stayed at home for three weeks healing, and I went back to work.

In the interim, we've downsized and moved just three blocks away from our "mansion" to our "mini-mansion," a much more affordable living arrangement for me. And when it all finally seemed to be over, life was fabulous, simply magical once again because when you have health, and your loved ones with you, that's what life is all about.

Chapter 89

The White House

At the end of May 2003 Chad received an email from the CureSearch, the National Childhood Cancer Foundation, based in Washington, D.C. and California. They'd heard about Chad's story on the brain tumor support list on the internet and wanted to know if he could perform for their conference on Capitol Hill in June. They told us that the honorary guest of the conference would be First Lady, Laura Bush. While driving to the conference I received a phone call on my cell. CureSearch wanted to know if Chad was prepared to perform a magic trick for Mrs. Bush.

"Absolutely. Chad's always prepared."

The first night of the conference Chad did "strolling" magic at the Welcome Reception. The next morning we were whisked away to a private room where Chad was prepared to perform for Mrs. Bush. My parents came with Faith so not to miss this exciting moment. There Mrs. Bush addressed an audience telling about the milestones being made in pediatric cancer research. And then she shared our story with the audience. Afterwards, she asked Chad to come forward and perform a magic trick for the audience to see.

When Chad finished his trick, she looked into the audience, straight at me and said, "Penny, you're the magic. You're always doing for everyone else. What can I do for you?" I was speechless for a few moments.

I know. I found it hard to believe, too.

Finally, I replied "Mrs. Bush, there's nothing. As long as my kids are healthy I'm the happiest woman in the world." Mrs. Bush told me to think about it some more and let her know. Then she invited Chad to be the magician at the Easter Egg Roll on the White House lawn. Every Easter Monday the White House has a huge Easter egg hunt for approximately 20,000 children. Another big break. We were ecstatic.

In the months that followed, Chad's career soared. He was the cover of all the local newspapers. Magazine articles were written about him. He developed his own website and made a DVD teaching simple magic. The Philadelphia 76ers and Philadelphia Flyers heard Chad's story and invited him to perform their games. The Philadelphia Eagles Fly organization heard his story and invited him to perform for their fundraising events. The malls started hiring Chad for different celebrations. The National Lymphoma and Leukemia Society hired Chad to perform in Epcot at one of their Team-in-Training events. All of Chad's magical wishes were coming true.

I would continually take Chad for MRI's, blood tests, and the like, and when the day was done, and all the tests were in, Chad was finally considered cured. He has his slight deficits from missing a piece of his brain, but basically, only his doctors and I notice.

And now look at him, my magical son. It was never easy for him so maybe that means the worst of it is over. From my mouth to God's ears.

After Don died, Chad decided he wasn't doing enough to honor his father's wishes of him becoming a professional magician. So he threw himself into the profession in earnest and as a result, he's performed for mayor's and magicians, presidents and first ladies, fund raisers, kids' birthday parties, big wigs at the casinos, and bigger wigs in Hollywood. But the most important are those performances for the kids now walking in the shoes Chad used to wear.

A few months after Don died, Chad was performing at a little boy's birthday party and the father approached me and said, "Where's his bracelet?"

"Huh?"

"This kid should have his own foundation. He's an inspiration. He's got a message to deliver."

Since one of Don's dying wishes was that Chad *spread the magic* across the world in the hopes that everyone would find it the way we did, we started the "Spread the Magic" Foundation, a NJ nonprofit organization that spreads magic to children with cancer in the hopes that they can find the magic in their life as Chad did. Chad, and I, as his mother, agent, scheduler, chauffer, choreographer, and producer have traveled to countless destinations all over the country and parts beyond, performing magic in hospital rooms and at campsites such as Paul Newman's Hole in the Wall Gang Camps, Ronald McDonald Camp, in Aruba for the ill children of the island, at fund raisers and festivals and anywhere else that will have us. Many of these kids for whom Chad performs are terminal, and tough as it may be for Chad to face that kind of crowd, he does it with charm and in great spirits. The fact is, he's the most inspirational, motivational, exuberant individual I've ever met, and because of it, the magic is spreading, just like Don wanted.

Although originally schooled by his best friend – Don – the follow up lessons have been with some of the world's greatest magicians. His mentor, Joe Holiday took over magically where Don left off. He counts Lance Burton, Johnny Thompson and Criss Angel among his friends; they've spent many hours giving him private tutorials and expanding his magical world. What a blessing.

And it hasn't stopped there. Chad, who loves to be on stage, had always dreamed of being on the big stage: Las Vegas. In 2006, he appeared with his friend, Lance Burton, along with the man who made this particular dream come true, Criss Angel. Like Lance, Criss is a superstar among magicians, doing crazy, unbelievable stunts that leave even the professionals scratching their heads. Criss Angel's dad also died of cancer and being that they were both magicians, I think they shared a special bond because of it.

So there we were in Las Vegas. Criss and his crew worked with Chad on perfecting a routine and prepping him for his big night on the stage. Before it was all over, Chad appeared not only on Lance Burton's stage in Las Vegas – with his name shining brightly from on the marquis at the Monte Carlo – but Criss Angel ran a special episode about Chad on his show, *MindFreak* on the A&E Network.

Wow! What a dream come true.

Chapter 90

Mono a Mono

Even as late as 2006 Chad had some physical ailments that rose levels above a cold or flu and had me running back to CHOP, my heart in my mouth once again. In June 2006 Chad started complaining of his stomach hurting, then his glands, then both at the same time. I poo-poo'd it for weeks because there was no way my baby would ever be sick again. He was the miracle, remember?

But one day in early June, Chad was performing for the kids at my school when a few of the teachers remarked how incredibly thin he looked and how white his coloring was and how he was sweating profusely. The Principal gave me permission to leave and I took Chad to the doctor's office immediately. Once again I was in panic mode and once again alone. My parents had retired and were living full time in Florida so I had no one to cry to.

The doctor who examined him said "Honestly, Penny, I'm concerned. His spleen is enlarged, his lymph nodes are swollen. This could be a relapse. He has all the signs. Take him to the emergency room immediately and get a CBC stat and a CAT scan of his organs."

For the fifth time in my life I was pleading with doctors, making deals with God, shaking all over and questioning God and Don as to why. Life had been so good for the past three years, and we were living our and then zap, right back into the world of doctors and needles and scans. None of us slept well that night.

The next morning the doctor called me.

"Penny, it's not cancer, its mono."

I almost collapsed from relief. The symptoms were so similar, but thankfully, magically, the blood work proved the best diagnosis. Chad had a weird virus, something that might take weeks or even months to recover from, but except for a lot of sleep time, he would be fine. We cancelled a few bookings, a few conventions, and a trip. Chad rested and once again, healed, once again stood up and performed yet another trick. Over the next few years Chad has many episodes of swollen lymph nodes as that's pretty common for cancer survivors whose immune system is still sluggish.

Chad. He's a dictionary entry next to the word magic. He sees only the good in people, the magic that each and every one of us has to bring to the world. Having seen life from both sides, the living and dying ones, he's always thrilled to still have his. He gets what's unimportant and works what is. He's my strength, and my hero. And he still worries me every third moment of every day.

Chapter 91

Keeping the Faith

She's got curly hair and round luscious lips that people pay money for, yet she's the most modest woman I know. Over the years she's learned to deal with her myriad losses – they started when she was so young – and has risen above the fray. Still when Self-Pity makes an appearance, you're likely to hear her lament the fact that Don won't be there to share this or that future moment: Daddy won't be here for my prom, graduation, wedding, fill in the blank.

I try to tell her that he will, that he'll be standing right there next to here every step of the way, that she might not be able to see or feel or touch him, but that his spirit has never left us. Cold comfort for a woman who's missing her daddy, who needs to feel blood pulsing beneath fingertips, a five-o'clock shadow as it brushes her cheek, a strong arm to steady weak knees. But it's the best advice I can give on limited resources.

And yet, she blossoms. After Don died, Faith took all her pain and threw it into her school books. She graduated top of her class from high school and went on to Rutgers as her dad wished for her. It's where she is today. Her boyfriend and best friend, Arthur, lived in the same dorm at Rutgers as Faith did. He shares her passion for tennis and the unfortunate experience that his father died of non-Hodgkin's lymphoma eighteen months before Don. Arthur's father, Arnold, and Don had been tennis partners. Faith and Arthur are like Don and I were: together since high school and very tight. What a terrific support system they are to each other.

Faith played on the high school tennis team for four years. Before she graduated, she formed the Dr. Don Juros Memorial Tennis Scholarship as her dad wished. She's focused, responsible, practical and trustworthy. She's a daughter and a confidant. My heart swells when I see what a beautiful woman this, my oldest child has become. Through all this adversity comes the rarest bloom, like a desert flower, not only surviving, but thriving.

In May 2004, before Faith started at Rutgers she got a phone call from the Jewish Federation of Atlantic County. She was chosen to be an Avoda Scholarship finalist and had to go in for an interview. She shook their hands and sat down and they asked her to recount her essay in her own words.

"But those *are* my words. I wrote that essay," she said.

"We know. Tell us again."

So she did, and when she finished chronicling her father's life and hers. because of it, there wasn't a dry eye in the place. And when they asked what her father would have thought about her going to Rutgers.

"It was his dying wish for me. It's my first choice. I don't just want to go, but I feel compelled to go. Then I'll have made all my father's dying wishes for me come true, just like my brother has. Now we only have my mother. She hasn't been able to yet, but she's trying."

Faith was awarded the scholarship and so began her college career. She graduated Rutgers University with high honors once again. She completed an internship at the college and taught a class there, "From Backpacks to Briefcases," a class about making the adjustment from high school to adulthood. Her big dream is to be Dean of a college someday, but for now she plans on becoming a CPA. Faith was hired at one of the big four accounting firms and over a year in advance they hired her for their auditing department, she made that great of an impression on them.

She's quiet and studious and unlike her brother, doesn't need to be the center of attention. She loves a good debate, and like Don, loves to be challenged and, like Don, always rises to the occasion. Ironically in her freshman year she was placed in the same exact dorm Don lived in. Divine intervention? Who knows? We chose to believe it was Don working his magic again. She didn't make that request yet there she was, living among her father's memories.

She still misses Don terribly and has some lingering guilt about those last days when he wanted to go out on "dates" with her and she frequently pushed him away. She didn't want the special attention then. She knew why it was happening and thought she could end-run Death by turning him down. When he'd ask if he could hold her hand she'd say no so he'd hold her elbow. He'd ask her to dance at her friends' bar and bat mitzvahs and she'd be embarrassed because none of her friends were dancing with their fathers so she'd say no. Now she wishes she'd said yes. *Oy*. Guilt wins this round.

Faith will prevail in whatever path she chooses to do in life. She's strong, like her father, and her mother, and she'll find her way. Of this I have no doubt.

Chapter 92

The End of the End

As for me, I'm doing what I was born to do: to be a mom; to provide a safe environment for my kids so they can live without the constant fear of loss and abandonment. Through the years we've had our moments, but we've survived. Heck, we've even done pretty well for ourselves, considering.

I took a job at my children's school district as an aide to the children with special needs. The students are terrific, and maybe because I know they're not dying, I don't find their conditions to be overtly sad. I enjoy helping them with reading and math and the job affords me my summers, nights and weekends off to run around with Chad if he needs me, and travel with him on vacations. Faith's got her own gigs going now, so I manage Chad's professional career, and act as his agent and as the CEO of the "Spread the Magic" Foundation. I've had a long-term relationship since Don died, hundreds of first meetings, very few first dates, and could write another book about the experiences I've had and the people I've met being single again.

A few years ago I met a widower with his own horribly painful story to tell. Michael and I found there was much to love and admire about each other. He wines me and dines me and buys me funny cards and walks with me on the boardwalk and enjoys the beach as much as I do. Together we travel to warm and sunny Siesta Key, Florida and are each other's partner in life. His family and mine are thrilled that we found each other after all our pain and losses. I make him laugh. And that's all I'll say on the subject given that the rest of the story's not been written yet. Perhaps I'll be able to make Don's wish for me come true, perhaps not. You can only put one foot in front of the other every day and hope that things turn out for the best. Either way, you learn to live with the result so no sense stressing it as you go. I've really had a pretty good life, the yucky, nasty brushes with death parts notwithstanding, and don't feel the need to ask for too much more.

This story is not a new story, it's not the first story, and neither will it be the last story, but it's my story, and I felt compelled to tell it, even if it does nothing more than provide a frame of reference for people walking this same road, the road that I stumbled down for nine long years. Although my husband died, both of my children are healthy now and in the long run that's what matters most – that the magic Don and I created is thriving. I miss Don terribly still, but I've found that there's always something missing in everyone's life, no matter how picture perfect it may look from the outside. I speak with him often throughout the day, visit his grave, sometimes bring a picnic lunch and share with him what's new in our life. But he already knows since he's orchestrating it all from above. I truly believe he died so Chad could live. And now, he's our guardian angel, protecting us from whatever he can. He died to watch over us and make sure that all of us will smile again, together in the forever, however long that may be.

At the end of this journey, I discovered that there's a reason why we're not prescient, why we can't see the future coming, or we'd dread it like a condemned building does the wrecking ball. We can't handle the future, despite the fact that we're always blindly rushing to it. And with all that rushing we miss the good things, the wonderful moments that make up every day if only we're open to seeing them. I take more time now for those moments. As for the rest, I'm still debating His/Her wisdom in all of it, and you can be damn sure I'll have a few questions about it when it's my turn to ask.

In the interim, I'm using my time wisely, rebuilding myself, my life, my family and those aspects of my world over which I have some measure of control, and which, truth be told, are infinitesimal.

Cherish yesterday, dream tomorrow, live today. That's lesson number one and the motto in which I taught my children to live by. I have a plaque saying the quote above my bed. You don't get these days back. Not a single one. So work them, full out, to the best of your ability with all your senses completely wide open and your mind on full alert. There will be a quiz.

Lesson number two: Live the Magic. Look closely at your life and you'll see it. There's magic in every single moment. For me it only took several life-changing, earth-shattering events to see it clearly. May you have better luck?

Lesson number three: Keep the Faith. I know I did. She brings me joy and pure pleasure.

And that's what this story's about. Three little lessons that make all the difference in the world. I guarantee if you wrap your arms around those babies your life will be the better for it.

As for the rest – its history, my history, and you are welcome to it if it helps you.

Not the happily ever after I'd dreamed of, but a decent compromise all things considered.

Chapter 93

Just You and Me

President's Day, 2007. My first baby was making the break. Faith had been offered an internship near her college which meant she would no longer be living at home during the summers. So she gave me her blessing to sell her furniture and turn her bedroom into a guest room/office. Since I had the day off, I decided to go furniture shopping. As I pulled into what would be the first of about fifteen furniture stores that day, it hit me with a sudden fierce, yet quiet force: I really was alone.

The last time I shopped for furniture was with Don. Not physically, mind you, but he had been alive, playing cards with Chad while tumors multiplied in his frontal lobes, and despite his condition, he'd been available for consultation. Not today though, and I didn't want to do this without him. Seven years had passed and I still missed him, still longed for him to be with me and share life's stuff. I blinked back a couple tears and walked into the store.

After two seconds inside, literally, *Just You and Me*, by Chicago came on the radio. That had been our song for twenty-four years! I was paralyzed with such emotion that I stopped dead in my tracks. I knew Don was sending me a signal. He didn't want me on this mission alone and was letting me know he was with me.

A salesman approached me to offer his assistance. I halted him with a raised hand, found the closest chair, closed my eyes and listened. For those precious few minutes I was sixteen again,and back on the dance floor with the man who would one day become my husband. For those precious few minutes, my Don was alive, infecting me with his laugh, enlivening the room with his beautiful smile. When the song ended I realized that no matter, no matter where, I was not alone in life, that Don would always be with me.

About four hours later and ninety minutes south of my first stop, I'm matching a pillow for color when out of nowhere; *Just You and Me* comes on the radio again. I couldn't believe my ears. I mean, what were the odds? The song's over thirty years old, for God sakes, and here it was on the radio twice in one day on two different radio stations. This time I smiled big, no tears, a mood I took with me when I left the store.

But my day of shopping with Don wasn't over yet. I stopped for dinner and was perusing a magazine and thinking about the exhausting, yet incredibly fun day I'd spent shopping with Don, when – you know what's coming – *Just You and Me* came on the radio for the third time that day. Now I was totally blown away. I stopped in mid-chew and just cried.

I looked up toward the sky and said out loud, "Thank you, Don, for this lovely date. I know no matter where I am in life you're always with me, from beginning to end."

Can you believe it? It's all true. I'm still blown away by it. What a gift he was to me.

I slept like a baby that night, cradled as I was, in the arms of love.

Now that's true magic.

ABOUT THE AUTHOR

Penny Juros lives in southern New Jersey close to the ocean. She is the proud mother of Faith and Chad. Penny works in the public school system and is the CEO and Executive Director of the Spread the Magic Foundation, a NJ nonprofit that spreads magic to children with cancer in the hopes that they can find the magic in their life as Chad did. She is also the manager to Chad's incredibly rewarding and entertaining magic career. You can learn more at www.magicalchad.com and www.spreadthemagic.org.